IRELAND

BY CARLA MOONEY

Essential Library

An Imprint of Abdo Publishing
abdobooks.com

ABDOBOOKS.COM
Published by Abdo Publishing, a division of ABDO, PO Box 398166, Minneapolis, Minnesota 55439.

Printed in China.
052025
092025

Cover Photo: Patryk Kosmider/Shutterstock Images, (castle); Marina Storm/Shutterstock Images (pattern)
Interior Photos: Alexey Fedorenko/Shutterstock Images, 4–5; Shutterstock Images, 6, 7, 10, 12–13, 24 (globe), 26–27, 28, 29, 36–37, 40, 54–55, 56, 74, 82, 85, 86–87, 90, 95, 101; Pavel Voitukovic/Shutterstock Images, 14–15; Sean O' Dwyer/Shutterstock Images, 18; Steve Allen/Shutterstock Images, 21; Markus Mainka/Shutterstock Images, 23; Red Line Editorial, 24 (map); Sanit Fuangnakhon/Shutterstock Images, 31; Marius Roman/Moment/Getty Images, 34; Irina Wilhauk/Shutterstock Images, 38–39, 88–89; Archive Photos/Getty Images, 42; Claudine Van Massenhove/Shutterstock Images, 47; Topical Press Agency/Hulton Archive/Getty Images, 49; Independent Newspapers Ireland/NLI Collection/Independent News and Media/Hulton Archive/Getty Images, 50; Marco de Benedictis/Shutterstock Images, 51; Dan Chung/AP Images, 52; Artur Widak/NurPhoto/Getty Images, 57; Bettmann/Getty Images, 59; Lipnitzki/Roger Viollet/Getty Images, 60; Joe Maher/Getty Images Entertainment/Getty Images, 62; Liudmyla Chuhunova/Shutterstock Images, 65; Brendan Moran/R&A/Getty Images, 66; Damien Storan/Shutterstock Images, 68–69; Damien Storan/PA Images/Getty Images, 70; Fabrizio Troiani/Alamy, 76; JoeFox/Radharc Images/Alamy, 78–79; Eric Isselee/Shutterstock Images, 83; Brian Lawless/PA Images/Getty Images, 93; iStockphoto, 97; Niall Carson/PA Images/Getty Images, 98

Editor: Marie Pearson
Series Designer: Maggie Villaume

Library of Congress Control Number: 2024948606

PUBLISHER'S CATALOGING-IN-PUBLICATION DATA
Names: Mooney, Carla, author.
Title: Ireland / by Carla Mooney
Description: Minneapolis, Minnesota: Abdo Publishing, 2026 | Series: Essential library of countries | Includes online resources and index.
Identifiers: ISBN 9781098296988 (lib. bdg.) | ISBN 9798384919506 (ebook)
Subjects: LCSH: Geography--Juvenile literature. | Ireland--Juvenile literature. | Europe--Juvenile literature. | Ireland--History--Juvenile literature.
Classification: DDC 949.5--dc23

CONTENTS

CHAPTER **ONE**

A TOUR OF IRELAND

It's evening when the plane touches down at Dublin Airport, several miles outside Dublin, Ireland. Daniel stretches his legs after the long flight across the Atlantic Ocean from Boston, Massachusetts. He slips his backpack over his shoulders and follows his parents into the bustling airport. Dublin Airport is Ireland's largest and busiest airport, with nearly 32 million passengers passing through its terminals in 2023.[1] Daniel is excited to visit Ireland and learn about his Irish heritage.

A taxi carries Daniel's family from the airport to a hotel in Dublin's city center. His older brother, Thomas, is waiting for them in the hotel lobby. Thomas has worked in accounting at a Dublin company for the past

The River Liffey starts in the Wicklow Mountains and flows east through Dublin.

two months. The family checks into the hotel. After getting a good night's sleep, everyone is ready for Thomas to show them around Dublin.

IRELAND'S CAPITAL CITY

Dublin is Ireland's capital city. It sits on Ireland's eastern coast at the head of Dublin Bay, an inlet of the Irish Sea. Approximately 25 percent of Ireland's population lives in the Greater Dublin area.[2] The River Liffey runs through the city center, and O'Connell's Bridge connects the city's northern and southern sides. The city is home to a mix of old and new, from Georgian buildings dating to the 1700s to modern concrete and glass office buildings. Throughout Dublin's streets, plentiful pubs and restaurants provide social gathering spots for residents and visitors alike.

Daniel's family walks a few blocks from the hotel to the nearest bus stop. The city streets are crowded with pedestrians walking to their destinations, while cars and buses travel on the city's roads. The Dublin Bus network connects different parts of the city. A light-rail system called the Luas connects Dublin's city center to its suburbs. Following Thomas's direction, they board a bus that carries them to their first stop: Dublin Castle.

DUBLIN PORT

Dublin's location on the coast has made Dublin Port the largest freight and passenger port in Ireland. Nearly 50 percent of Ireland's trade flows through the port.[3] Dublin Port is also located near a hub for Ireland's train and roadway networks, making it a key part of moving people and goods throughout the country.

Dublin Castle includes the Chapel Royal, which opened in 1814.

For centuries, Dublin Castle has stood in the heart of Dublin. It stands on elevated ground that formerly held a Viking settlement. Construction of Dublin Castle began in 1204 by order of King John of England. The king initially built the castle as a medieval fortress with four corner towers connected by high walls surrounding a large courtyard. From 1204 until 1922, Dublin Castle also served as a residence for the British monarch's representative in Ireland. After a large fire damaged much of the fortress in 1684, the castle was rebuilt from the late 1600s into the 1700s and transformed into a Georgian palace, including a suite of grand reception rooms called the State Apartments.

These rooms hosted balls, banquets, and ceremonies. After Ireland gained independence from the United Kingdom in 1922, the Irish government held state ceremonies, dinners, and commemorations on the castle's grounds. Each Irish president is inaugurated in Dublin Castle's St. Patrick's Hall.

The family leaves Dublin Castle and heads to a nearby pub for lunch. Daniel decides to order one of Ireland's traditional dishes, Irish stew. The stew is a steaming bowl filled with pieces of lamb, potatoes, onions, celery, carrots, leeks, and various herbs such as thyme and rosemary. On the side is a classic dish of mash, the Irish version of mashed potatoes. Thick slices of buttered bread also accompany the stew. It's delicious, and he eats every last bite.

After lunch, Daniel's family strolls through Dublin's city streets. They pass several places and landmarks that Daniel has read about, including the world-renowned Trinity College (Ireland's oldest college), the Ha'penny Bridge, St. Patrick's Cathedral (Ireland's largest cathedral), and the Guinness Storehouse, where visitors can learn about how Ireland's famous beer is made. The family

HA'PENNY BRIDGE

The Ha'penny Bridge is a well-known landmark in Dublin. Opened in 1816, the bridge was the first pedestrian bridge across the River Liffey. For the first ten days, people could walk the bridge for free. After that, they had to pay a toll in ha'pennies, which were British coins. Although the bridge's official name is the Liffey Bridge, the bridge's toll history led to its nickname, the Ha'penny Bridge.

stops to take a quick picture beside the famous Molly Malone statue, which depicts a well-known woman from Irish folklore whose ghost is said to haunt Dublin since her death a long time ago. She serves as a symbol of the city. Daniel can't wait to spend more time at these places in the coming days.

ANCIENT BRÚ NA BÓINNE

Daniel and his family rent a car the next day and drive to the peaceful Boyne Valley, about 30 miles (48 km) north of Dublin.[4] Daniel explores one of Ireland's most ancient sites in the Boyne Valley: Brú na Bóinne. Located near the River Boyne, Brú na Bóinne is famous for its prehistoric passage tombs of Newgrange, Knowth, and Dowth. Archaeologists estimate that the tombs were built more than 5,000 years ago as a place to bury kings and perform sacred rituals. In recognition of their significance to human history, Brú na Bóinne has been designated as a United Nations Educational, Scientific and Cultural Organization (UNESCO) World Heritage site.

An average of 30,000 people walk over Dublin's Ha'penny Bridge every day.[5]

Daniel and his family start their visit at the Brú na Bóinne Visitor Center. From there, they board a shuttle bus to Newgrange. Built around 3200 BCE, Newgrange is older than Stonehenge in England and the Great Pyramids of Giza in Egypt. From the outside, Newgrange looks like a massive earth-and-stone mound. A grass dome sits on top of white, round stone walls. The stone

The Newgrange mound is 43 feet (13 m) high and 279 feet (85 m) across.

walls showcase detailed carvings with spirals, geometric patterns, and animal motifs. As Daniel studies the fascinating carvings, he wonders about the meaning and significance behind each of these ancient works of art.

A guide leads Daniel and the other visitors inside the Newgrange mound. The entrance is guarded by a large carved stone with double and triple spirals. Above the entrance, a slit called a roof-box lets light into the mound. A narrow passage lined with stone boulders leads into a central tomb chamber with several recesses. In each recess, there are large basin stones that would have held cremated human remains and funeral offerings such as beads and pendants.

Inside, the guide demonstrates one of the tomb's most remarkable features: it may have been designed to act as a calendar. Each year just after sunrise on the winter solstice from December 18 to 23, sunlight shines through the roof-box and illuminates the long passage into the central tomb chamber for 17 minutes.[6] Daniel is fascinated as the guide simulates the winter sunrise, and a light illuminates the ancient carvings within the tomb.

After their visit to Ireland's ancient past, Daniel and his family drive back to Dublin. As the sun

WORLD HERITAGE SITES

World Heritage sites are places worldwide that have natural or cultural importance. They are chosen by UNESCO. Once an area is selected as a World Heritage site, it is protected. There are more than 1,000 World Heritage sites globally.[7] Cultural sites include historic buildings, archaeological sites, and significant works of art. The three main prehistoric sites of the Brú na Bóinne—Newgrange, Knowth, and Dowth—are designated as World Heritage sites in Ireland. They hold Europe's largest and most significant collection of large, prehistoric stone art.

Dún Aonghasa is the ruins of a 3,000-year-old fort whose history and dramatic setting attract many visitors.

sets, the family settles into the hotel for the night. They have big plans for the next day: an early morning round of golf at the famous Portmarnock Golf Club, which has hosted many golf championships over the years. It's sure to be another memorable experience in Ireland.

IRELAND: THE EMERALD ISLE

Visitors from around the world travel to Ireland every year. From the rugged Cliffs of Moher to the lively city of Dublin, Ireland's sights attract people of all ages and interests. Ireland, sometimes called the Republic of Ireland, is a small country on an island west of Great Britain. The island of Ireland is divided into two parts: the Republic of Ireland and Northern Ireland, which is part of the United Kingdom. Ireland is home to more than 5.2 million people.[8] That is about 1.5 percent of the population of the United States.[9]

Ireland's lush landscapes and rolling hills in shades of green have earned it the nickname the Emerald Isle. Ireland is a beloved travel destination for many, known for its beautiful scenery, rich history, and vibrant culture. The Irish are fond of saying *"Erin go bragh!"* This means "Ireland forever!"

CHAPTER **TWO**

GEOGRAPHY

Ireland is known for its rolling hills and beautiful green landscapes. Across the country, picturesque meadows mix with rocky mountains and dramatic cliffs to create memorable settings. Ireland's natural beauty draws new and returning visitors to the island nation.

Ireland is located on an island in the North Atlantic Ocean, west of the island of Great Britain. It shares the island with Northern Ireland, a separate country that is part of the United Kingdom. Three bodies of water surround Ireland. The North Atlantic Ocean lies to the west, while the Celtic Sea borders Ireland in the south. The Irish Sea lies to the east and separates Ireland from the island of Great Britain.

Ireland is a relatively small country, with a land area of 26,596 square miles (68,883 sq km). It is

The Iveragh Peninsula is famous for its breathtaking scenery, including streams and hills. This mostly rural region provides many opportunities to enjoy the outdoors.

about the size of West Virginia. Ireland measures approximately 171 miles (275 km) east to west at its widest point. From its southernmost tip to its northern point, Ireland stretches 302 miles (486 km).[1]

Ireland's coastline features numerous peninsulas, which are areas of land surrounded by water on three sides and connected to the mainland on one side. The Dingle Peninsula is a popular destination on Ireland's southwestern coast, extending 30 miles (48 km) into the Atlantic Ocean.[2] On the peninsula, cliffs rise above sandy beaches along the coastline. Mountains run down the peninsula's center, including Mount Brandon, the country's second-highest peak. Other large peninsulas include the Iveragh Peninsula, Beara Peninsula, and Inishowen Peninsula.

Many smaller islands are scattered throughout the seas that surround Ireland. People lived on many of these tiny islands until the late 1800s. Today only a handful of these islands have permanent residents. Achill Island, located west of Ireland's mainland, is the largest of the smaller islands, with a coastline stretching almost 80 miles (129 km).[3] Other notable islands include North Bull Island near Dublin, Lambay Island off the eastern coast, and the Aran Islands chain on Ireland's Atlantic coastline.

RING OF KERRY

The Ring of Kerry is a 111-mile (179 km) driving route around the Iveragh Peninsula, showcasing many of Ireland's breathtaking landscapes.[4] On the route, visitors travel through Ireland's forests to the Atlantic coast. They view rugged mountains, flora and fauna, waterfalls, lakes, and sandy beaches. The route's natural beauty has made it one of Ireland's most popular destinations.

LOWLANDS AND MOUNTAINS

Ireland occupies about 80 percent of the island it shares with Northern Ireland.[11]

Across the island, Ireland's landscape includes an area of central plains and lowlands surrounded by hills and jagged mountains. The interior of Ireland is composed mainly of lowlands. These are defined as areas of land less than 492 feet (150 m) above sea level.[5] Ireland's central lowlands are primarily made of flat plains, though they also have low, rolling hills.

Rolling hills and low mountains surround Ireland's central lowlands. More than 30 mountain ranges rise across Ireland, most of them in coastal regions. Ireland's highest mountains are in the southwest, with several peaks reaching more than 3,000 feet (914 m).[6]

Ireland's tallest mountain range is Macgillycuddy's Reeks, also known simply as the Reeks, located on the Iveragh Peninsula in southwestern Ireland. The range includes Ireland's tallest peak, Carrantuohill, which rises 3,415 feet (1,041 m).[7] Carrantuohill is popular with hikers and mountain climbers. There are several other tall peaks in the Reeks, including Beenkeragh at 3,308 feet (1,008 m) and Caher at 3,300 feet (1,000 m).[8]

Ireland's Wicklow Mountains in the country's southeast stretch from County Dublin north into County Wexford. Lugnaquilla Mountain is the tallest peak in the Wicklow Mountains. It measures 3,035 feet (925 m).[9] The second-highest peak in the mountain range is Mullaghcleevaun at 2,780 feet (847 m).[10] The area around the mountain range has been designated a national park,

People can hire a guide to help them climb Carrantuohill. It can take seven to ten hours to climb and descend the mountain.

the Wicklow Mountains National Park. The park is a popular destination for hikers and others who enjoy outdoor recreation, from fishing to camping, cycling, hang gliding, rock climbing, off-roading, and more.

DRUMLINS

As the ice covering Ireland during the last Ice Age started melting around 27,000 years ago, it left behind sediment deposits. These deposits became smooth, oval-shaped hills of varying sizes

THE BURREN

In County Clare, the Burren is a memorable landscape of exposed limestone rock. Horizontal slabs of limestone are separated by channels formed by water over long periods. Several underground rivers flow through the Burren. In some areas, the water has eroded the limestone to form caves. The Burren is an example of a karst landscape, a type of landscape formed when rain and groundwater dissolve limestone.

called drumlins. The name *drumlin* comes from a Gaelic word meaning "rounded hill." They look like half-buried eggs, with a steeper side and a lower, sloping side. Many drumlins are found across Ireland in groups called fields or swarms, making the landscape look like a rolling blanket.

Ireland's drumlins are made of deposits of silt, gravel, sand, soil, and boulders. Some drumlins have solid rock at their core. All the material was left behind by retreating glaciers. The drumlins' rounded shape formed when melting ice moved over them. Scientists study drumlins to learn about Ireland's geological history and how glaciers and ice sheets moved. The drumlin's lower sloping side points in the direction that the glacier moved.

LAKES AND RIVERS

Across Ireland, there are more than 12,000 lakes. Ireland's lakes and reservoirs provide most of the country's drinking water. Lough Corrib, the country's largest freshwater lake, lies in western Ireland's Counties Galway and Mayo. It covers an area of 68 square miles (176 sq km). This deep lake reaches about 164 feet (50 m) below the surface at its maximum depth.[12] It holds about

211 billion gallons (800 billion L) of water.[13] That is enough water to fill more than 300,000 swimming pools. Lough Corrib also holds more than 300 small islands.[14] Other major lakes include Lough Derg, Ireland's third-largest lake, and Lough Leane. According to legend, Lough Leane in southwestern Ireland's County Kerry holds Tír na nÓg, the land of eternal youth, under its surface.

Several rivers flow through Ireland's cities, towns, and countryside. Rivers have long been essential in transporting goods and people, providing water and food, and being a habitat for wildlife. Ireland's longest river is the River Shannon, which begins in County Cavan in the north and travels 224 miles (360 km) before flowing into the Atlantic Ocean near Limerick.[15] The River Shannon is the main river running through Ireland's central lowlands. Marshes, bogs, and lakes line the river along much of its length. The River Barrow is Ireland's second-longest river. It flows 120 miles (193 km) from the Slieve Bloom Mountains in central Ireland and empties into the Celtic Sea at Waterford.[16] The River Barrow is part of a trio of rivers, along with the Rivers Nore and Suir, called the Three Sisters.

PEATLANDS

Ireland has many dense wetlands known as peatlands. Peatlands are swampy areas filled with partially decayed plant matter, called peat. Bogs are a common type of peatland in Ireland. Bogs previously covered as much as 5,000 square miles (13,000 sq km) of Ireland.[17] That's about one-fifth of Ireland's land.[18] They formed thousands of years ago when the ice sheets covering Ireland began to melt, leaving behind ridges. Tiny, shallow lakes formed in places where the melting water

Ireland's peat bogs are made of dead plant matter, but they are also home to many species of plants and animals.

was trapped. Plants grew around these lakes, and as the plants died, their remains built up to become a layer of peat. Eventually, these tiny lakes became bogs.

Today, there are two main types of bogs in Ireland: raised bogs and blanket bogs. Raised bogs formed as dead plants slowly filled the Ice Age lakes. Blanket bogs developed in Ireland's mountains and along the western coast. These bogs formed in areas where the soil drained poorly and it was very rainy. The peat covered large areas of land like a blanket.

COASTAL REGIONS

Ireland has a coastline about 900 miles (1,448 km) long.[19] The country has shores along the Atlantic Ocean, the Irish Sea, and the Celtic Sea. Busy seaports, scenic fishing harbors, sandy beaches, and stunning cliffs meet the sea at the land's edges.

Ireland's coastline is not smooth. The jagged coastline is broken up by inlets, peninsulas, and bays. Towering cliffs overlook the sea in several areas, especially along the Atlantic coast. Some of the most famous Irish cliffs are the Cliffs of Moher, which span nearly five miles (8 km) along the Atlantic coast in western Ireland's County Clare.[20]

CLIFFS OF MOHER

The Cliffs of Moher are one of Ireland's most spectacular geographic features. The sheer cliffs tower as far as 702 feet (214 m) above the Atlantic Ocean at their highest point.[22] From the cliffs, one can see as far as the Aran Islands in Galway Bay. Walking paths along the cliffs connect the towns of Liscannor and Doolin and provide many scenic views. The cliffs have appeared in several popular movies, including *Harry Potter and the Half-Blood Prince* and *The Princess Bride*.

CLIMATE IN IRELAND

Ireland has a temperate oceanic climate with mild winters and cool summers. The country rarely experiences extreme hot or cold temperatures. In the winter, temperatures typically range from 39.2 to 45.7 degrees Fahrenheit (4–7.6°C). Summer temperatures typically range from 54.1 to 60.3 degrees Fahrenheit (12.3–15.7°C).[21]

Rainfall across Ireland is abundant, with the highest rainfall in the west and in areas with high elevations. The country's average annual rainfall is about 48 inches (122 cm), but high elevations

Visitors can catch spectacular views from O'Brien's Tower along the Cliffs of Moher. The tower was built in 1835.

MAP OF IRELAND

KEY:

- Capital
- City
- Point of Interest

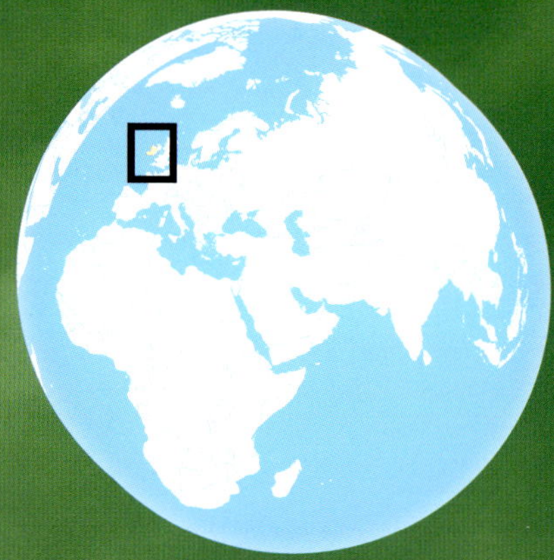

may experience as much as 118 inches (300 cm).[23] Spring and summer are the driest times of the year, while autumn and winter are typically wetter.

Several factors affect Ireland's climate, including ocean currents and air masses. An air mass is a large amount of air that is mostly uniform in temperature and moisture level. The North Atlantic current carries warm water from the South Atlantic Ocean to Ireland's western coast. The winds moving from the southwest spread warm air, creating mild winters, especially in western Ireland.

IRELAND'S BIOME

Ireland's biome is a temperate deciduous forest. A biome is a community of plants and animals that adapt to and live in a specific climate. Around the world, there are five major biomes: aquatic, grassland, forest, desert, and tundra. Within the forest biome are three major types of forests: tropical, temperate, and boreal (taiga). In Ireland's temperate forests, there are well-defined seasons and a moderate climate. Most forest trees are deciduous, which means they lose their leaves in the fall.

Thousands of years ago, Ireland was covered with woodlands. However, humans cleared Ireland's native cover. By the early 1900s, only about 1 percent of Ireland's forests remained.[24] Today, small areas of forest are scattered across the country.

CHAPTER **THREE**

PLANTS AND ANIMALS

Ireland is home to a diverse assortment of life. More than 31,000 species of plants, animals, fungi, and other organisms live in Ireland.[1] They each have their own habitat needs.

Various habitats across Ireland provide places for plants, animals, and other organisms to live. A suitable habitat meets an organism's needs for survival. For animals, a habitat must include food, water, shelter, and mates for the animals to reproduce. For plants, a habitat needs the right amount of light, air, and water and the right type of soil. Ireland's diverse habitats include woodland forests, grasslands, marshes, peat bogs, fens, freshwater and coastal habitats, rocky mountains, and more.

Deer can be spotted in Ireland, including in Killarney National Park.

WOODLAND FORESTS

Thousands of years ago, about 80 percent of Ireland's land was covered with woodland forests.[2] Elm, hazel, and ash trees grew in the eastern lowlands, while oak and hazel trees grew in the western lowlands. Scots pine and birch trees grew at higher elevations, while alder and willow trees thrived in marshes. Over centuries, humans cleared many of Ireland's original woodland forests for producing lumber and for farming.

By the late 1800s, only about 1 percent of Ireland's land was forested. Tree-planting initiatives have enabled Ireland's woodland forests to recover a bit, growing across about 11 percent of the country's land.[3] However, Ireland is still one of the least-wooded countries in Europe.

Today, most trees across Ireland are spruce trees. For decades, the Irish government paid landowners to plant trees on their land. Many of those landowners planted spruce trees because they grow fast and could be harvested for timber in only 15 years. Ireland's native broad-leaved trees, including oak, ash, birch, hawthorn, and hazel, grow on approximately 2 percent of the country's land.[4]

HAWTHORN LEGEND AND LUCK

The hawthorn tree is small with thorny branches and thick foliage. In Celtic legend, the hawthorn tree is part of the fairy tree triad with oak and ash trees. Fairies will be found where the three trees grow together. Today, some people in Ireland believe the hawthorn tree marks a meeting place for humans and fairies. Others believe it will bring good luck and fortune. As a result, many Irish people will not cut down a hawthorn tree.

In wetlands, sphagnum moss grows close together, making a carpet on the ground.

WETLANDS

Wetlands cover nearly 15 percent of Ireland.[5] A wetland is an area where the ground is very wet most of the time. Thousands of wetlands big and small are scattered across Ireland and include marshes, peat bogs, fens, and swamps. They provide essential habitats for many species of plants and animals.

There are more than 4,000 species of plants in Ireland.[8]

Ireland is well-known for its bogs. Over many years, the bogs slowly filled with plant debris. Plants such as sphagnum moss grew around a bog's edges and spread across the entire bog. The sphagnum moss created the bog's thick, spongy carpet, which floats on layers of wet, partially decayed plant material.

Today Ireland's bogs are home to a variety of plant species. Commonly growing in bogs along with sphagnum moss are bog cotton, butterwort, and heathers. Bog cotton blooms in fluffy white bunches in the spring and summer months, while heathers provide purple cover across Ireland's bogs, moors, and mountains. Carnivorous butterwort plants attract and trap insects.

GRASSLANDS AND HEATHLANDS

Grasslands are the most common habitat across Ireland, covering more than 60 percent of the country.[6] They are home to many grass species, including bent grasses, meadow grasses, meadow foxtails, fescues, and cattails. Other plants, wildflowers, and shrubs such as heath rushes, sedges, heathers, hawthorns, and gorses are also common in Ireland's grasslands.

Heathlands cover a little more than 2 percent of Ireland.[7] Dry heathlands are broad, open areas with grasses and low-growing shrubs such as gorse, heather, and bilberry. Heathlands formed when humans cleared the land for agriculture or forestry activities. However, farming was eventually abandoned on these lands because the soil was unsuitable for agriculture.

THE IRISH SHAMROCK

Ireland's national plant is the shamrock, a small three-leaf clover. In Celtic legend, the shamrock could be used as a charm to protect against evil. Saint Patrick was a Catholic Christian missionary to Ireland in the 400s. He used the shamrock to teach people about the God of Christianity. According to Christianity, God exists as three distinct persons: the Father, Son, and Holy Spirit. Together, these three persons are united as the one God. According to legend, Saint Patrick explained this with a shamrock, which has three leaves but is one shamrock. This illustration helped spread Christianity across Ireland. Several clover species are considered shamrocks, all of which grow across Ireland.

Shrubs began growing there instead. There are also a few wet heathland areas located low on the slopes of hills and mountains, where plants such as heath, heather, and sphagnum moss are more common.

COASTAL REGIONS AND OTHER HABITATS

Ireland's coastal regions have many habitats for plants and animals, including cliffs, rocky shores, sandy beaches, dunes, salt marshes, and more. These diverse coastal habitats are home to various plants and animals. The species that live in these habitats have adapted to survive in a highly salty environment.

The common glasswort is one type of plant that grows in the salt marshes near Ireland's coasts. The plant has a stubby green stem and branches that bloom with tiny flowers during late summer and early fall. Various types of seaweeds can be found along the Irish coast, including kelp, dulse, and carrageen. Many seaweeds are actually not plants at all but species of algae. Found along the Irish coast, kelp is a type of algae. Instead of a stem, kelp has a structure called a holdfast that supports the kelp as the tide flows around it.

ANIMALS IN IRELAND

Various animal species live in Ireland. During the Ice Age, several large species roamed across Ireland, including mammoths, Irish elk, and a species of brown bear. As the ice melted, Ireland became an island separated from mainland Europe. As a result, animals could no longer move freely between Ireland and Europe. These large mammals are no longer found in Ireland, and scientists believe that human hunting may have caused their disappearance.

Today, 26 land mammals are native to Ireland, including the Irish hare.[9] Irish hares are known for standing up on their hind legs and appearing to box, a ritual part of their mating behaviors. Other small mammals such as the red fox, hedgehog, pygmy shrew, Irish stoat, and badger are also commonly seen across the country. Less commonly spotted native animals include the red deer and pine marten.

IRISH STOAT

The Irish stoat is a species widespread across Ireland and related to the weasel. The small mammal has a long, thin body, short legs, and a flat head. Its fur is chestnut colored with a creamy underbelly. It can swim, climb, and slip into underground burrows. The stoat lives alone and hunts prey such as rabbits, rats, pygmy shrews, mice, and more. In Connemara in western Ireland, the Irish stoat was called *Beanín uasal*, meaning "noble little woman," because some believed the small mammal was a witch in disguise.

Sea mammals such as dolphins and whales swim along the Irish coastline. Several species of dolphins, including the bottlenose dolphin, Risso's dolphin, common dolphin, and harbor porpoise, swim near Ireland, especially along the southern and western coasts. Several species of whales have been spotted in Irish waters, including humpback whales, blue whales, minke whales, fin whales, sperm whales, and pilot whales. If they are lucky, visitors may spot a humpback whale lifting its tail out of the water. Seals also live in Ireland's seas.

A variety of fish and other species live in the waters in and around Ireland. These other marine animals include dogfish, sunfish, lobsters, crabs, eels, and mackerel. Ireland's freshwater lakes and rivers are home to otters, salmon, trout, pike, Arctic char, pollan, eels, crayfish, and more.

Only three species of amphibians are native to Ireland: the common frog, natterjack toad, and smooth newt. The common frog is widespread across the country and lives near lakes, rivers, and other bodies of water where it can feed and mate. Common frogs are brown, green, and yellow. Their long hind legs and webbed feet help them jump, swim, and escape predators. The natterjack toad is similar to the common frog, but it has shorter legs and a yellow line that runs down its back. The natterjack toad is rare and one of Ireland's most endangered species. The smooth newt is a brown lizard-like amphibian that is commonly spotted in Ireland's garden ponds. It hibernates in winter under dead wood, beneath stones, and among tree roots.

There are no snakes on the island of Ireland. Only one native reptile species is found there—the common lizard. This lizard lives in bogs, coastal regions, and grasslands. It preys on insects, snails, and spiders. Like many reptiles, it hibernates in winter and emerges in the spring to mate.

Atlantic puffins can be found on the Skellig Islands.

Ireland is home to more than 400 bird species.[10] The country is a frequent stopping place for birds migrating from the Arctic, Africa, and North America. In the fall, birds such as sandpipers, pipers, and warblers arrive from North America and make temporary homes in southern Ireland. Birds migrating from Africa, including shearwaters and auks, arrive in the spring and go to southwestern Ireland. Seabirds such as herring gulls and gray herons are common along the country's rugged coastlines, while puffins, which look similar to penguins, live in large colonies on

Ireland's coastal cliffs. Other common birds across Ireland include the robin, house sparrow, blue tit, and starling.

More than 11,500 insect species live in Ireland.[11] Scientists discover new insect species every year. Dragonflies and spiders are common in Ireland's bogs. Butterflies such as the common blue butterfly and meadow brown butterfly flit among wildflowers in grasslands. Other widespread insects include the emperor moth and the common field grasshopper.

NATIONAL PARKS AND CONSERVATION

Across Ireland, there are six national parks, each of which plays a role in preserving landscapes, habitats, plants, and animals. The largest national park is the Wicklow Mountains National Park, located south of Dublin. The park's protected lands cover more than 79 square miles (205 sq km), including mountains, blanket bogs, woodlands, streams, and lakes.[12] Many native mammal species, such as deer, foxes, badgers, and hares, can be spotted in Wicklow Mountains National Park. Peregrine falcons and hawks, along with several other bird species, are often seen flying high above the park.

Along with its national parks, Ireland has 77 nature reserves.[13] These reserves protect critical areas for plants, animals, and habitats and provide scientific research and study opportunities. The Irish government owns most reserves, but private organizations and individuals own a few.

In 2022, scientists warned that one-quarter of Ireland's native species were at risk of extinction, or dying out. The director of Ireland's National Biodiversity Data Center, Dr. Liam Lysaght, named

Wicklow Mountains National Park has nine marked trails for visitors to explore.

human activity as one of the main threats to Ireland's species. For example, the population of the herring gull has declined by 90 percent over the past 30 years, according to Lysaght.[14] The director attributes the bird's decline to human disruption of its natural marine habitat through overfishing and climate change, which have decreased the gulls' food supply.

Lysaght said other species at risk in Ireland include the Atlantic salmon, the European eel, the freshwater pearl mussel, and the great yellow bumblebee. The reduction or loss of a species can have a ripple effect across its ecosystem. For example, yellow bumblebees perform the essential job of pollinating flowers, fruits, and vegetables. As the number of yellow bumblebees declines, there may not be enough pollinators left to grow an adequate supply of fruits and vegetables.

CHAPTER **FOUR**

HISTORY

Over thousands of years, Ireland has had a complex history of conflict, culture, and religion. The country's history begins in prehistoric times, long before written records existed. Archaeologists have uncovered evidence that early humans arrived in Ireland around 12,500 years ago. These people were hunter-gatherers. They survived by hunting animals and gathering wild plants and other needed resources. Most lived a nomadic lifestyle, moving from place to place throughout the year in search of food.

Around 4000 BCE, the first farmers appeared in Ireland. Early farmers domesticated cattle, sheep, goats, and pigs. They grew early versions of wheat and barley plants. They cleared large forests of oak and elm trees

Poulnabrone Dolmen is a portal tomb that dates to more than 5,000 years ago. It includes a capstone propped up over the entrance.

Carvings such as those at Newgrange show glimpses of the lives of ancient people.

to create spaces where they could plant crops and allow their livestock to graze. Often, they chose sites close to a reliable water source.

With farming, the people no longer had to move from place to place to find food. Reliable food and water sources meant they could stay in one place for a long time. Many gradually abandoned the nomadic lifestyle and built permanent settlements. They supplemented their farming diets with hunting and gathering wild foods.

The early farmers built large stone tombs for their dead, also known as megalithic tombs or passage tombs. Many passage tombs were built in a round mound on a hilltop. The people decorated the tombs with stone carvings. The people also used these stone monuments as places for other religious ceremonies during the year. One of Ireland's most well-known prehistoric stone monuments is Newgrange in Brú na Bóinne.

EARLY CELTIC IRELAND

Historians believe that the Celts arrived in Ireland from mainland Europe around 500 BCE, and they likely continued to arrive over the following several hundred years. The Celts were divided into separate tribes or clans. However, these different groups shared a similar culture. The Celtic tribes brought their religious traditions, customs, and language to their new home in Ireland.

A Celtic tribe was led by a chieftain who ruled over the tribe's territory, made trade decisions, and led warriors in battle. Celtic warriors protected the tribe and territory and enforced the laws. The Celtic people worshipped several gods and goddesses, each of which ruled over an aspect of life and the natural world. The Celts viewed nature as sacred, with certain places such as mountains or springs having religious importance, and they held festivals to celebrate changing seasons.

Over time, the Celtic language evolved into the modern-day Irish Gaelic language. The Celts had no written records. Instead, they passed down information from generation to generation through oral storytelling. This rich storytelling tradition continued to be used for Irish myths and legends.

Legend says that Saint Patrick removed all snakes from Ireland.

EARLY CHRISTIANS IN IRELAND

Beginning around 400 CE, Christianity arrived in Ireland. At the time, most people in Ireland believed in many gods and goddesses. The first Christians to set foot in Ireland were likely missionaries from Britain.

One of the most famous missionaries was Saint Patrick of Britain. After being enslaved in Ireland and escaping, Patrick became a cleric in Britain. He later returned to Ireland around 432 as a Christian missionary. Saint Patrick and other missionaries worked to convert the Celts to Christianity and established churches and places of worship across Ireland.

In Ireland, Christianity merged with existing local customs and traditions. For example, some Celtic sites were turned into Christian places of worship, while Celtic symbols such as the sun cross were used in Christian images.

Blending new religious traditions with familiar customs helped people accept Christianity. By 500, most people living in Ireland were Christians. Monasteries, the homes of religious men called monks, became important centers of learning and art. Monks created intricate illuminated manuscripts, which are handwritten books decorated with rich, hand-painted colors. The *Book of Kells* is a famous illuminated Christian text created by monks in Ireland.

THE VIKING AGE

The first Vikings from Scandinavia reached Ireland's shores around 795. The Vikings plundered islands off Ireland's northern and western coasts. Over the next 200 years, the Vikings raided Irish settlements and monasteries along the coasts and along Ireland's major rivers. In each raid, they took valuable religious items and enslaved people.

The Vikings' influence had a lasting impact on Ireland. Several Viking settlements, such as Dublin, Waterford, and Wexford, became some of Ireland's first urban centers in the 900s. The Vikings also introduced new trade routes from Ireland to the Byzantine Empire and Asia. Traders brought back bars or blocks of silver and gold that were melted down to make various decorative ornaments

IRELAND'S HIGH KING

Born around 941, Brian Boru rose to become the king of Munster and later the high king of Ireland, uniting the Irish kingdoms. Boru's most significant achievement occurred at the Battle of Clontarf in 1014, when his forces defeated Viking forces. The victory triggered the downfall of the Viking military in Ireland but came at a great price, as Boru was killed during the battle.

and jewelry. However, the Vikings' influence declined after the defeat of a Viking force at the Battle of Clontarf, near Dublin, in 1014.

ANGLO-NORMAN INVASION

In 1169, a group of Anglo-Norman invaders from England arrived in Ireland. These mighty warriors fought to control land in Ireland. A few years later, King Henry II of England landed in Ireland and declared his rule over the country. The invasion began hundreds of years of British rule and conflict in Ireland.

Over the next several centuries, the Anglo-Normans built castles and towns across Ireland. They introduced the British legal system. They also formed bonds with the Irish people and adopted Irish customs and language over time.

By 1300, the Anglo-Normans controlled much of Ireland, except for a few territories in the west. The British lords established an area known as the Pale in parts of what are now the counties of Dublin, Louth, Meath, and Kildare. British rule was followed in the Pale, but the Irish people still followed Irish customs and laws outside the Pale.

In the 1500s, the British monarchy attempted to assert greater control over Ireland. In 1542, King Henry VIII of England declared he was the king of Ireland. He attempted to force the Irish clans to surrender their lands to the British. If they wanted their lands returned, the Irish clans would have to give up their language, customs, laws, and religion and follow the British king. These policies led to revolts and uprisings against the British Crown.

One of the most significant uprisings was the Nine Years' War (1593–1603), when the Irish lords of the northern province of Ulster fought British rule but were eventually defeated. After putting down the uprisings, the British government seized lands from the Catholic Irish lords. They gave the land to Protestants from England and Scotland. Protestantism and Catholicism are both branches of Christianity, and most Irish people were Catholic. The most significant resettlement of land occurred in Ulster. This transfer of land would sow the seeds of future division between the Protestants and Catholics in Northern Ireland.

Ireland has more than 30,000 castles and ruins.[1]

STRUGGLE FOR CONTROL

The struggle for control of Ireland continued in the 1600s. In 1641 the Irish rebelled against British settlers. Britain's Oliver Cromwell and his army arrived in Ireland in 1649 to put down the rebellion. Cromwell's forces massacred thousands of Irish people and burned and raided communities as they moved through the country. After Cromwell's victory, the British claimed large swaths of Irish land and gave them to British soldiers and citizens.

In 1695 the British passed the harsh Penal Laws, rules that were designed to strengthen the power of British Protestants in Ireland. These laws banned Catholics from practicing their religion and closed Catholic schools. The Penal Laws also banned the use of the Irish language and prohibited the Irish people from voting, working for the government, or holding public office.

Changes to the Penal Laws began being made in 1778, making them less strict. The laws were eventually removed entirely in 1829.

UNREST GROWS

In the 1700s, the Penal Laws restricted the rights and opportunities of Irish Catholics, while British Protestant power continued to grow. In 1789 the Society of United Irishmen led a rebellion against the British. The rebellion was unsuccessful, but the dream of Irish independence had left its mark. Unrest continued to grow in the 1800s.

In 1801 the Act of Union created the United Kingdom of Great Britain and Ireland, called *Britain* for short. The British Parliament completely replaced the Irish government. The British government in London now governed Ireland along with Scotland and Wales. Ireland was granted the right to send representatives to the British Parliament's House of Lords and House of Commons.

THE GREAT FAMINE

By the mid-1800s, more than eight million people lived in Ireland.[2] Many relied on the potato as a staple food because it was nutritious and easy to grow. However, beginning in 1845, a disease known as potato blight destroyed the potato crop over multiple years.

The loss of the potato crop was catastrophic for Ireland and caused the Great Famine. Farmers without crops could not feed their families or pay their rent. Despite the shortage, the British government did not restrict exports and provided inadequate relief to Irish farmers.

Statues in Dublin stand in remembrance of the victims of the Great Famine.

More than one million people died of starvation and disease. Another two million left Ireland, many immigrating to the United States.[3] By 1851 the Irish population had dropped to fewer than six million people.[4] Today, Ireland's population has still not returned to prefamine levels.

FIGHTING FOR INDEPENDENCE

In the late 1800s and early 1900s, the Irish struggle for independence intensified. Irish people developed the Home Rule movement, which pushed for Ireland to self-govern while remaining part of Britain. However, Protestant unionists in Ireland's northern regions disagreed. They wanted to remain under British rule.

On Easter Monday, April 24, 1916, an armed insurrection attempted to overthrow British rule in Dublin. The rebellion, later known as the Easter Rising, was unsuccessful. On April 29, the leaders surrendered. The British executed many of them. The violent British response turned Irish public opinion in favor of independence.

In 1918 the Irish political party Sinn Féin formed an Irish Parliament. It declared Ireland's independence from Britain and formed the Irish Republican Army (IRA). In 1919 the Irish War of

IRISH IN AMERICA

After leaving Ireland, many Irish people landed in the United States. An estimated six million Irish people have immigrated to the United States since 1820.[5] Between 1820 and 1860, one-third of all immigrants to the United States were Irish.[6] In the years before Ireland's Great Famine, most Irish immigrants to the United States were male, but during the famine, entire Irish families made the long voyage to the United States. Today, one out of every six Americans claim Irish heritage.[7]

Independence (1919–1921) began. Members of the IRA, led by Irish rebel Michael Collins, carried out attacks against British forces including ambushes and raids. The IRA wanted to force the British to negotiate with its members, granting independence to Ireland.

Eventually the two sides came to an agreement with the Anglo-Irish Treaty of 1921. The treaty called for six counties in the northeast to become Northern Ireland and remain part of Britain. The remaining 26 counties in Ireland became the Irish Free State, a self-governing territory that remained part of the British Commonwealth.

Disputes over the treaty led to the Irish Civil War (1922–1923). Some accepted the treaty, while others pushed for Ireland to become a full republic. During the hostilities, Collins was assassinated. A ceasefire in 1923 ended the civil war. However, the separation of the mainly

More than 1,400 people, including hundreds of civilians, died in the Irish Civil War.

MINI **BIO**

MICHAEL COLLINS

Michael Collins was one of Ireland's pivotal figures in the fight for Irish independence. Collins was born in 1890 in Clonakilty, County Cork, to a farming family. Upon completing his schooling, Collins took a job with the post office. He spent nine years in London, where he became involved in the movement for Irish independence. In 1909 Collins joined the secretive Irish Republican Brotherhood, an organization dedicated to Irish independence.

In 1916 Collins was part of the Easter Rising armed rebellion. After it failed, he was jailed for a few months by the British. Collins went into hiding in 1918 to avoid being conscripted into the British military. Later that year, he won a seat in the Irish Parliament. In 1919 the Irish Parliament declared itself independent of Britain, and Collins was appointed a minister in the Irish government.

When the Irish War of Independence broke out in 1919, Collins led members of the IRA against the British. After a truce was reached in 1921, Collins led the Irish at the peace conference that produced the Anglo-Irish Treaty of 1921, which created the Irish Free State. However, when the Irish Civil War broke out between pro-treaty and anti-treaty sides, anti-treaty fighters assassinated 31-year-old Collins in an ambush in 1922.

Michael Collins was known as a strategic leader.

Protestant, pro-British Northern Ireland and the primarily Catholic, pro-independence Ireland created a long-standing conflict between the two communities that would flare up in future years.

AN INDEPENDENT REPUBLIC

The Irish people ratified the Constitution of Ireland in 1937. The constitution, written in Irish and English, established the country's government and courts. It also described the rights granted to every Irish citizen. While many countries became involved in World War II (1939–1945), Ireland remained neutral, a foreign policy the country still follows.

In 1949 the Irish Free State declared itself a fully independent republic, the Republic of Ireland. It was no longer part of the British Commonwealth. The Republic of Ireland joined the United Nations in 1955 and the European Union (EU) in 1973.

EUROPEAN UNION

In 1973 Ireland joined the EU. The EU is a political and economic alliance of European countries. It was formed to strengthen European economic and political cooperation after World War II. The EU requires its members to follow specific laws about trade, security, immigration, and environmental regulations.

THE TROUBLES

The conflict between Northern Ireland, where many Protestants wanted to remain part of the United Kingdom, and Ireland, where many Catholics believed in a united, independent Ireland, simmered for years. In the late 1960s, violence

Irish prime minister Bertie Ahern, *left*, and British prime minister Tony Blair, *right*, signed the Good Friday Agreement. US senator George Mitchell, *center*, helped chair the talks.

broke out in Northern Ireland between the two sides. Riots, street fighting, bombings, and sniper attacks occurred in Northern Ireland.

This 30-year period of violence and conflict was known as the Troubles. One side, the Unionists, wanted Northern Ireland to remain part of the United Kingdom. The Nationalists wanted Northern Ireland to become part of Ireland. The conflict was often violent, and terrorism from both sides led to more than 3,600 deaths and tens of thousands of injuries.[8] An agreement made on Good Friday, April 10, 1998, ended the violence. The Good Friday Agreement was a compromise that established relationships between the United Kingdom, Northern Ireland, and Ireland. It also established the Northern Ireland Assembly, which brought the two sides together to handle local matters. Since the agreement, the island has been mostly peaceful.

Ireland's history has been shaped by the people who have landed on its shores over the centuries. From its early Celtic roots to a modern independent republic, Ireland has evolved throughout its history while maintaining a distinct identity and culture. In recent years, the country has successfully dealt with challenges such as the global coronavirus pandemic starting in 2020, recording one of the lowest coronavirus death rates in Europe through January 2023. Proud of their past, Ireland and the Irish people are looking forward to the future.

CHAPTER **FIVE**

PEOPLE AND CULTURE

The people of Ireland have a rich culture that has roots in the country's history. Over the years, the Celts, Vikings, Anglo-Normans, and British came to Ireland and brought their unique traditions and cultures. Over time, these cultures have left their imprint on Ireland and its people.

Approximately 5.2 million people made their home in Ireland in 2024.[1] Ireland ranks 124th in population among all countries.[2] The median age of the Irish people is 40.2 years, making it one of Europe's younger populations.[3] Ireland's population is slowly growing, and its birth rate of 11.1 births per 1,000 people gives the nation the ninth-highest birth rate in Europe.[4]

People in Dublin have access to plenty of shopping, including the high-end Grafton Street shops.

Ireland has the highest proportion of redheads in the world, estimated at more than 10 percent of the population.

In 2022, 76.6 percent of the people in Ireland were of Irish heritage. The other main ethnic groups in the country included non-Irish white at 9.9 percent, Asian at 3.3 percent, Black at 1.5 percent, and other or unspecified at 4.6 percent. This last category included people of Arab, Roma, and mixed ethnicities. Irish Travellers make up 0.6 percent of the population.[5] Irish Travellers are indigenous to Ireland and traditionally lived as nomads, moving from place to place.

Ireland is in the lower half of European countries for population density. There was an average of 198 people per square mile (76 per sq km) in 2024.[6] In comparison, France and the United

Kingdom have higher population densities, with France at 316 people per square mile (122 per sq km) and the United Kingdom at 741 per square mile (286 per sq km).[7]

Some 64.5 percent of Ireland's population is concentrated in urban areas, particularly on the eastern side. The largest concentration of people is found in and around the capital city of Dublin on Ireland's eastern coast, where about 1.27 million people live.[8] Other large cities in Ireland include Cork, Galway, Limerick, and Waterford. The western areas of Ireland, where there are fewer job opportunities and transportation options, have fewer people.

Immigrants have had an important role in Ireland's growing population in recent years. Approximately 12 percent of Ireland's population was born elsewhere and immigrated to Ireland.[9] Many immigrants came from the United Kingdom, Poland, Lithuania, India, and Brazil.

In 2021, Syrian, Somali, Kenyan, and Libyan activists participated in the Parallel Peace Project, which included a light show that highlighted the female immigrants in Ireland whose lives have been affected by war.

LANGUAGE

The official languages of Ireland are English and Irish. English is widely spoken across the country, although the accent differs from that of American English. Most schools, businesses, and organizations use English as their primary language.

Irish, also known as Gaeilge or Gaelic, is a Celtic language spoken by about 37.7 percent of people in Ireland.[10] The Irish language is most commonly spoken in small towns and villages along Ireland's western coast. In recent decades, the Irish government has encouraged the use of Gaelic, with schools and communities teaching the language. Some Irish authors, such as Nuala Ní Dhomhnaill and Cathal Ó Searcaigh, write only in Irish.

Irish immigrants to the United States brought the Irish language with them. Over time, some Irish words have been incorporated into American English. For example, words such as *shenanigans* and *slew*—meaning "a large number"—come from the Irish language.

RELIGION

Christianity is the largest religion in Ireland, with nearly 76 percent of the population identifying as Christians. There are several denominations of Christianity in Ireland. A significant majority of Irish people, 69.2 percent, are Roman Catholic, with smaller numbers of Protestants at 3.7 percent, Orthodox at 2 percent, and other Christians at 0.9 percent. A small percentage of people in Ireland practice non-Christian religions, including Islam at 1.6 percent and other non-Christian religions at 1.4 percent. Nearly 15 percent of Irish report that they do not practice any religion.[11]

As guaranteed by the Constitution of Ireland, citizens and residents of Ireland are granted religious freedom and can practice any faith. But the Catholic Church runs about 90 percent of primary schools across Ireland and about 50 percent of secondary schools.[12] The Catholic Church also runs many hospitals in Ireland. However, the connection between the Church and the Irish state is declining. The Irish government has adopted policies opposed by the Catholic Church. For example, Ireland made divorce legal in 1997 and approved same-sex marriage in 2015.

JAMES HOBAN

James Hoban (1762–1831) was an Irish-born architect. Hoban studied to become an architect in Dublin and immigrated to the United States in the 1780s. He worked in Charleston, South Carolina, before winning a contest to design the White House (pictured) in Washington, DC, in 1792. Hoban's design was influenced by Leinster House in Dublin. Hoban supervised the restoration of the White House after the British burned it during the War of 1812. He also oversaw several other significant buildings in Washington, DC, including the US Capitol.

ARTS AND LITERATURE

Ireland has made numerous contributions to literature, art, music, and more. Famous Irish writers have written classic pieces of literature enjoyed worldwide, including author Bram Stoker, who wrote *Dracula*, and Frank McCourt, author of the Pulitzer Prize–winning *Angela's Ashes*, which covers his childhood in Limerick. Irish author James Joyce is regarded by many as one of the most influential

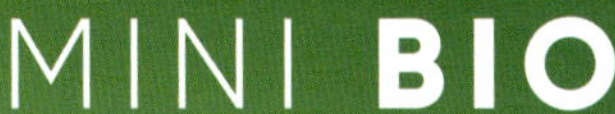

JAMES JOYCE

James Joyce is praised as one of the most influential writers of the 1900s. Born in 1882, Joyce grew up in Dublin as the oldest of ten children. Joyce did well in school. In 1898, Joyce attended University College Dublin, where he studied languages and literature and decided to become a writer. Throughout his college years and after his graduation in 1902, Joyce continually experimented with verse and practiced his writing craft.

In 1904 Joyce published several stories and began writing his novel *A Portrait of the Artist as a Young Man*. In 1907 Joyce published his first collection of poems, *Chamber Music*. Over the next two decades, he published the collection of short stories *Dubliners*, another collection of poems called *Pomes Penyeach*, and the novels *Ulysses* and *Finnegans Wake*, among other writings.

Over the years, Joyce has been recognized for his use of innovative language, dialogue, and frankness. Not everyone approved at the time, and his novel *Ulysses* was banned in the United States from 1922 to 1933. Joyce died in 1941 of complications from surgery.

James Joyce used a technique called stream of consciousness in *Ulysses*.

writers of the 1900s. Other well-known Irish novelists include Samuel Beckett, John Boyne, Maeve Binchy, and Jonathan Swift.

Ireland has also produced many famous poets, including William Butler Yeats and Katharine Tynan. Irish playwrights, directors, and actors have been featured on stage and screen worldwide. Oscar Wilde is a famous poet and playwright who wrote several plays that are still performed today, including *The Importance of Being Earnest*. A long list of notable Irish actors, such as Colin Farrell, Michael Gambon, Pierce Brosnan, Richard Harris, Cillian Murphy, and Saoirse Ronan, have entertained film and play audiences.

Irish composers and musicians have created contemporary music that people listen to worldwide. U2, one of the most famous Irish rock bands, formed in Dublin in 1976. Other well-known Irish musicians include Sinéad O'Connor, Enya, the Cranberries, and Niall Horan.

IRISH FOLK MUSIC AND DANCE

Along with contemporary music, Ireland is well-known for its traditional folk music. Irish folk music, often passed down from generation to generation, has played an important role in Irish culture. It is played in pubs, concert halls, and homes across Ireland. Some folk tunes are sung in English, some in Irish, and some in a mix of the two languages.

There are folk songs for many moods, from melancholy ballads to celebratory dance tunes. Instrumental folk songs are typically performed as fast jigs, reels, hornpipes, polkas, and marches. The fiddle is the most commonly played instrument in Irish folk music. Other instruments include

The *Riverdance* show features Irish music and dancing.

the wooden flute, tin whistle, uilleann pipes, concertina, and diatonic accordion. Musicians keep the beat with a frame drum, bones, or spoons.

While Irish folk music plays, Irish dancers often step onstage to perform. Irish dance is a form of traditional Gaelic dance. Irish dancers can perform alone or in groups, showcasing intricate footwork and steps while keeping their upper bodies stiff and not moving their arms or hands. Female dancers often wear short dresses in bright colors, while male dancers perform in shirts and trousers with brightly colored waist sashes. Irish dance is now popular worldwide, with people in many countries learning and performing the dance's quick steps.

PUB LIFE

Throughout the country, Irish pubs are a cherished part of the culture. Irish pubs, or public houses, do much more than serve food and drinks; they are central hubs for Irish life. Pubs are known for being warm and welcoming and often have a rich history in the community. The pub is traditionally a place where local people and visitors gather to share stories and comfort food, raise a pint of beer or glass of whiskey, and enjoy live music. For generations, the Irish have celebrated many of life's important events with family and friends at pubs, from weddings and christenings to wakes and funerals. The relaxed pub atmosphere brings people from all backgrounds together and builds lasting bonds.

Each Irish pub has its own character and is a reflection of the community it serves. Dimly lit, cozy interiors with warm fireplaces welcome locals and visitors and encourage conversations. Many pubs serve traditional Irish comfort foods such as stews, soda bread, and fish and chips. Live performances of traditional Irish music, called trad sessions, form an important part of pub life. Musicians gather and play tunes with fiddles, tin whistles, and other instruments, adding to a pub's lively atmosphere.

IRISH STORYTELLERS

Storytelling has a long history in Ireland, with origins in the nation's Celtic roots. In Celtic societies, storytellers called bards memorized poetry and songs and performed live. Without written records, the Celtic bards held and passed down the community's histories. Over time, bards became *seanchaí*, or storytellers who traveled from town to town to inform and entertain with ancient legends and cautionary tales. Today, the oral tradition continues in Ireland, with storytellers entertaining crowds with tales of Irish folklore and legends.

In recent years, many Irish pubs have incorporated modern elements. They offer craft beers, modern cocktails, nonalcoholic drinks, and gourmet food. Some pubs look to entice customers by hosting special events, holding karaoke nights, and providing board games.

But Irish pub culture can have a dark side. According to a 2023 study, about 82 percent of Irish adults had drunk alcohol in the past 30 days, with 47 percent of those adults engaging in alcohol misuse behavior. That includes binge drinking, or drinking at least six drinks in a day.[13] This type of drinking behavior can become a public health problem because regular alcohol consumption is a significant risk factor for a number of conditions, including alcohol addiction and liver disease.

IRISH WHISKEY

The history of Irish whiskey goes back centuries, with the first documented whiskey production in 1405. Irish whiskey brands such as Jameson, Bushmills, and Redbreast are enjoyed by people worldwide. In Ireland, distilleries offer tours and tastings of their whiskeys for locals and tourists alike.

FOOD

Irish food is known for being hearty comfort food. Traditionally, Irish food features simple ingredients grown or raised nearby. Irish dishes typically use staple ingredients such as potatoes, beef, lamb, seafood, cheese, and other dairy products. Potatoes remain one of the country's most popular menu items. Bread is also a staple of the Irish diet, especially soda bread and brown bread. Irish breads are often served with butter and hearty soups and stews.

The potato pancake known as a *boxty* is one of many uses for potatoes in Irish cuisine.

Ballybunion Golf Club is in southwestern Ireland on the Atlantic coast.

In Irish homes, one might eat a stew filled with lamb, potatoes, onions, carrots, and other root vegetables. Vegetable soups and seafood chowder are also popular comfort foods. Other traditional Irish dishes include *boxty*, a pan-fried grated-potato pancake, and colcannon mash, which is a mash of potatoes, kale, butter, and milk often served with sausages.

SPORTS AND RECREATION

Golf enthusiasts worldwide travel to Ireland's beautiful courses to play a round. Ireland hosts several golf tournaments yearly, including the Irish PGA Championship and the Irish Open. In 2027 Ireland was scheduled to host the Ryder Cup at Adare Manor. The Ryder Cup draws some of the best golfers in the world for a three-day competition between teams from the United States and Europe. Top Irish golfers include Padraig Harrington and Shane Lowry.

Hurling is another popular Irish sport. It requires speed and combines lacrosse, baseball, and field hockey skills. Teams of 15 play on a rectangular grass field with H-shaped goals at both ends. Players carry a stick called a *hurley* and use it to strike a ball called a *sliotar*. Players score three points when they hit the ball through the lower section of the goal into the net or one point when they send it over the crossbar. The team with the most points at the end of the match is the winner.

A sliotar ball hit during a hurling match can fly up to 112 miles per hour (180 kmh).[14]

CHAPTER **SIX**

POLITICS

In 1937 the Constitution of Ireland was enacted. The constitution established Ireland's system of government as a parliamentary representative democracy. Under this system, government power in Ireland is divided among legislative, executive, and judicial branches.

The constitution defines the powers of each branch of government. It prevents one branch from interfering with the operation of the other two branches. Ireland's president is the country's head of state, a largely ceremonial position. The people elect the president through a direct vote. Once elected, the president serves a seven-year term and is limited to two terms. Michael D. Higgins became Ireland's president in 2011 and was re-elected in 2018. His last term would be over after the 2025 election for Ireland's next president.

Ireland's parliament meets in the Leinster House in Dublin.

President Michael D. Higgins, *left*, met with Simon Harris, *right*, when Harris was appointed as taoiseach on April 9, 2024.

The president's powers are detailed in the Constitution of Ireland. The president appoints the taoiseach (prime minister), as well as government officials and judges. The president signs legislation into law and can refer bills to Ireland's Supreme Court for review. The president is also the supreme commander of the Defense Forces and represents the people of Ireland at events at home and worldwide.

THE LEGISLATURE: OIREACHTAS

Ireland's parliament, known as the Oireachtas, is the legislative branch responsible for making the country's laws. The Oireachtas consists of two houses: the Dáil Éireann (Lower House) and the Seanad Éireann (Upper House). Ireland's president is a member of the Oireachtas.

A member of the Dáil Éireann is called a *teachta dála* (TD). Citizens elect TDs to represent their interests in government. The number of TDs in the Dáil can vary, as the constitution requires at least one TD for every 20,000 to 30,000 citizens. In 2025 there were 174 TDs, an increase from the previous election.[1]

The Seanad Éireann has 60 members, called senators. The taoiseach, graduates from Ireland's universities, and panels of people who represent various vocational interests appoint senators. Sometimes, senators can be elected in a special Seanad election after the general election.

A proposed new law is called a bill. A bill must be debated and then voted on and passed in the Dáil and the Seanad in order to become a law. Once the bill passes both houses, the president signs it into law. Sometimes, a bill that does not pass the Seanad can still become law if the Dáil passes a resolution. The new law becomes an Act of the Oireachtas and is added to Ireland's Statute Book.

ELECTIONS IN IRELAND

Elections for TDs in the Dáil must be held at least every five years according to Ireland's constitution. Elections can occur more frequently if called for by the president, often in consultation with the taoiseach. To call for an election, the president dissolves the Dáil. The taoiseach can request at any time that the president dissolve the Dáil.

The president must dissolve the Dáil if the taoiseach has majority support in the Dáil. If there is not full support, the president can refuse. After dissolving the Dáil, a general election occurs within 30 days. All Irish citizens can vote if they are at least 18 years old by Election Day and registered to vote. Ireland is divided into constituencies, and each elects a minimum of three TDs. The number of constituencies can change when a Dáil is dissolved to account for an increase or decrease in population. To serve in the Dáil, a person must be an Irish citizen and at least 21 years old.

Most candidates running for office are part of a political party. The main parties are the Fianna Fáil, Fine Gael, and Sinn Féin. A few TDs are not affiliated with a political party and run as independents. The Fianna Fáil was founded in 1926 and is one of Ireland's oldest political parties. Party members generally hold centrist-conservative political views in Ireland's politics. The party supports conservative values and strongly supports Irish culture and identity. The party held 37 seats in the Dáil in 2024.[2]

> **LOCAL GOVERNMENT**
>
> In addition to the national government, Ireland has 31 county or city councils.[5] The councils are responsible for various local services, including housing, roads, libraries, and fire services. Citizens elect council members called councillors to represent their interests and make local policy decisions.

Founded in 1933, Fine Gael is a right-leaning political party that supports conservative values. The party believes in personal freedoms, individual responsibility, and free-market ideas. In 2024 the Fine Gael party held 35 of the 160 seats in the Dáil.[3]

Sinn Féin was founded in 1905 and had an essential role in Ireland's independence from Britain. It is a left-wing party that opposes British rule in Northern Ireland. The party advocates for a reunification of Ireland and supports social justice issues. In 2024 Sinn Féin held 37 of the 160 seats in the Dáil.[4]

FORMING A GOVERNMENT

After an election, the Dáil votes to choose the taoiseach. Usually the taoiseach is a member of the party that holds the most seats. If there is no clear majority party, two or more political parties may join together with independent TDs to build a coalition government. If the TDs cannot choose a taoiseach and form a government, the previous taoiseach may ask the president to dissolve the Dáil, and the election process begins again.

Once chosen, the taoiseach appoints TDs, usually from the majority party, to serve in the cabinet of ministers. The cabinet of ministers is also called the government. Each minister leads a department of the government with specific areas of responsibility. After the taoiseach nominates the ministers, the Dáil must approve them. The cabinet must have at least seven members and no more than 15 members.

EXECUTIVE

In Ireland, the taoiseach and that person's advisers hold executive power, which is the power to enforce the country's laws. The taoiseach is considered the head of Ireland's government and leads the majority political party in the Oireachtas. The Dáil nominates the taoiseach, and the president appoints them. There is no set term length for the taoiseach, but they must maintain support from the Dáil to remain in office. In April 2024 Simon Harris of the Fine Gael party was appointed Ireland's taoiseach.

The taoiseach is responsible for enforcing Ireland's laws and is assisted by the deputy prime minister and a cabinet of department ministers. The taoiseach, deputy prime minister, and all department ministers must be members of the Oireachtas.

GUARDIANS OF THE PEACE

Ireland's cities and towns do not have local police forces. Instead, a nationwide police force called the Guardians of the Peace was formed in 1922. The force includes a few hundred plainclothes detectives who may carry firearms. The uniformed police are unarmed. A commissioner leads the Guardians and reports to the country's minister for justice.

JUDICIARY

When Simon Harris entered office in 2024 at age 37, he became the youngest taoiseach in Ireland's history.

The third branch of Ireland's government is the judiciary. The judiciary or courts have the power to interpret the law. The judiciary is also responsible for determining whether a law passed by the legislature is unconstitutional. The president appoints judges at the recommendation of advisers. A judge cannot be removed from the bench unless both houses of the legislature pass a resolution to do so. Judges have a mandatory retirement age of 70.

Ireland's court system has five levels: the District Court, Circuit Court, High Court or Criminal Court, Court of Appeal, and Supreme Court. Each court hears different cases based on the type and level of the case. The Supreme Court is the highest court in Ireland. It hears appeals on the country's most important civil and criminal cases. It determines whether a law is unconstitutional.

In Ireland there are two main categories of court cases: civil and criminal. Civil cases are usually between individuals seeking to be paid or recover money. For example, a lawsuit for breaking a contract would be a civil case. The state brings criminal cases against individuals for breaking the law. A judge decides some minor criminal cases, while most serious cases, such as those involving murder, rape, and theft, are decided by a judge and jury.

When a case involves certain serious crimes such as terrorism or organized crime, it is sent to the Special Criminal Court. This court is intended for situations that regular courts are unable to deal with because of a high risk of jury intimidation. In recent years, the Special Criminal Court has

The Supreme Court of Ireland meets in the Four Courts building in Dublin.

heard cases involving organized drug activities. A Special Criminal Court has three judges who are appointed by the government from the High Court, Circuit Court, and District Court. There is no jury in a Special Criminal Court trial.

SPECIALIZED COURTS

Specialized courts deal with specific cases or defendants. The Children Court handles cases with charges against children under 16 years old, as long as the charges are not serious. The Children Court does not handle homicide cases. This specialized court can be held in the same courtrooms as District Courts or in different settings. Sometimes, the Children Court is called Juvenile Court.

The Drug Treatment Court handles cases for nonviolent offenders in Dublin. This court attempts to help people with substance abuse problems get treatment instead of putting them in prison. Through long-term, court-supervised treatment, offenders can address and treat their addictions and become law-abiding citizens.

MILITARY IN IRELAND

Ireland's military, called the Defense Forces, is made primarily of an army with a small navy and air force. The military has both active-duty and reserve personnel. They are all volunteers because there is no draft or conscription in Ireland. On December 31, 2023, there were 7,550 permanent active-duty military members, with 6,136 army personnel, 689 air force personnel, and 725 navy personnel.[6]

MILITARY NEUTRALITY

Since becoming an independent republic, Ireland has adhered to a policy of military neutrality. Under this policy, Ireland has not joined military alliances, including the North Atlantic Treaty Organization (NATO), a military alliance of several European and North American countries. Ireland has not participated in international conflicts and remained neutral during World War II. However, Ireland's military has participated in peacekeeping and humanitarian missions for the United Nations.

Under Ireland's constitution, the president is the military's supreme commander. However, in practice, the taoiseach directs Ireland's armed forces in consultation with the minister of defense and a defense council. Ireland's military has participated in United Nations peacekeeping missions in places such as Lebanon, Afghanistan, and the Balkans.

CHAPTER **SEVEN**

ECONOMICS

Ireland's official currency was once the Irish pound. But in 1999 Ireland became one of the first countries to use the euro. To use this new multicountry currency, Ireland became a member of the eurozone, a group of countries in the EU that use the euro as their official currency. After a three-year period of dual circulation of the Irish pound and euro, the euro permanently replaced the Irish pound starting in 2002.

The European Central Bank issues the euro, the second-most-traded currency on the world's foreign exchange markets after the US dollar. The euro is also a major global reserve currency. A global reserve currency is held in large amounts by central banks or other monetary authorities as part of their reserves.

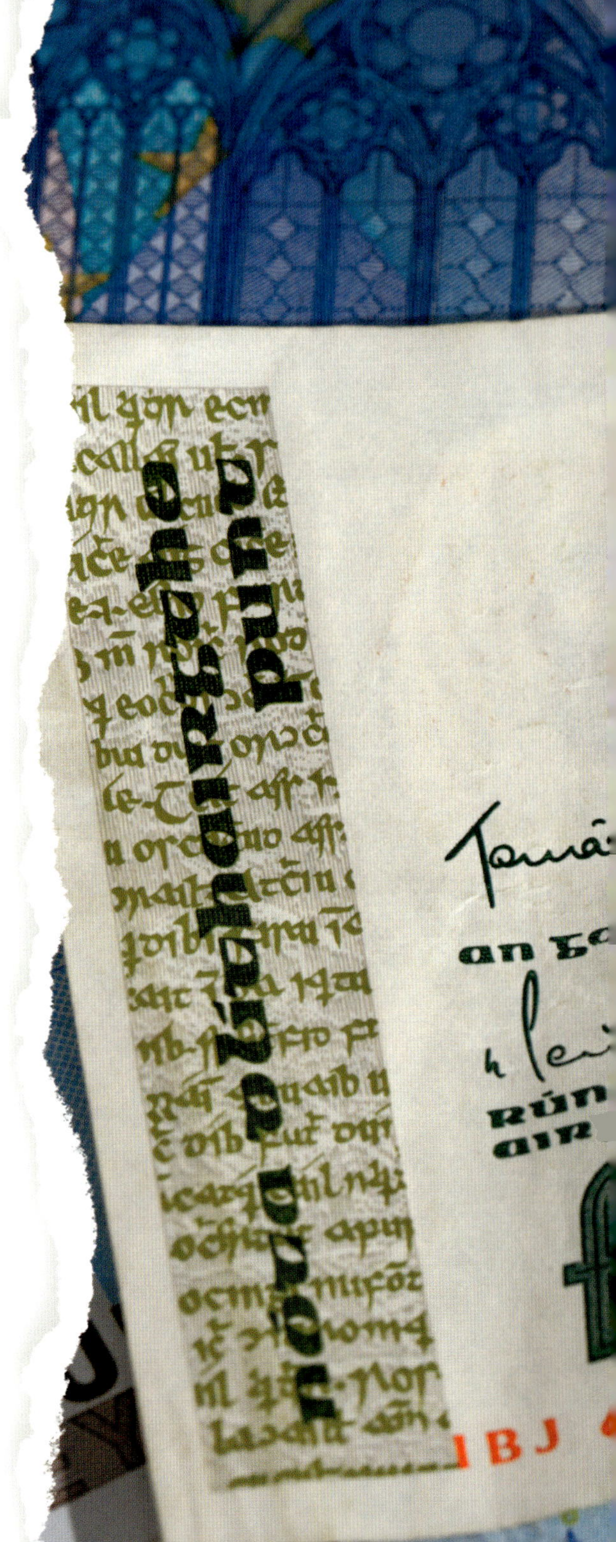

The old one-pound Irish note featured Medb, a queen from Irish mythology.

It can be used in international transactions and investments and is often considered a safe and stable currency.

MAJOR INDUSTRIES

Since the early 1900s, Ireland has transformed from a primarily rural agricultural economy to a diverse economy that has embraced technology and industry. In 2023 Ireland produced $545.63 billion in gross domestic product (GDP).[1] GDP is the income a country generates from the sales of goods and services in one year. It is a way to measure the economic strength of a country. When ranked by GDP, Ireland was the 26th-largest economy worldwide.[2] In 2023 Ireland's GDP per capita was approximately $103,685, well above the worldwide GDP per capita of $13,133.[3]

The service industry in Ireland is the largest contributor to its GDP. In 2022, services contributed 52.61 percent of GDP.[4] The service industry also employed 77 percent of Ireland's workforce.[5] One of Ireland's key service industries is financial services. Dublin has become a financial hub for Europe, with many international banks, insurance companies, and financial technology start-up companies having offices in the city.

TOURISM

Tourism has a significant role in Ireland's economy. In 2023, 6.3 million foreign visitors traveled to Ireland, according to Ireland's Central Statistics Office. Of those visitors, 41 percent came to Ireland for vacation, and 37 percent came to visit family or friends. The visitors spent $8 billion on their travels, which included hotels and other accommodations, transportation, entertainment tickets, and other daily expenditures.[6]

Ireland has low taxes for companies, and the nation has many skilled workers. For these reasons, several major technology companies, such as Google, Meta, and Microsoft, also have offices in Ireland, contributing to its technology and digital services sector. Tourism is another piece of Ireland's service industries. So are cybersecurity, data analytics, and e-commerce.

Manufacturing contributed 41.5 percent to Ireland's GDP in 2023 and provided about 19 percent of the country's jobs.[7] Some of the largest industrial sectors in Ireland include pharmaceuticals, biotechnology, and medical devices. Several large multinational corporations, such as Johnson & Johnson, Pfizer, and Boston Scientific, have industrial facilities in Ireland. Other growing industries include computer hardware and software, beverages and brewing, renewable energy, and information and communications technology.

Agriculture makes up a small part of Ireland's economy. It contributes about 1 percent of GDP and employs about 4 percent of Ireland's workforce.[8] Ireland is a major livestock producer and exports about 80 to 90 percent of its beef and dairy products.[9] Other livestock and crops include pork, chicken, lamb, barley, wheat, potatoes, oats, and rapeseed. Ireland's land and climate are unsuitable for large-scale production of grains and other crops, so the country imports about 80 percent of the food, beverages, and animal feed that it needs.[10]

The average visitor to Ireland in 2023 spent $1,276 on their trip and stayed an average of 8.2 nights.[11]

Fishing remains a smaller but still important part of Ireland's economy and society, especially for communities along Ireland's coasts. The clean ocean

In Ireland, cattle are raised for beef and dairy products. Most of these products are exported.

waters around Ireland have provided quality seafood for generations. In 2022, fishing generated $1.42 billion for Ireland's economy and provided more than 15,000 jobs.[12] Top-selling fish and seafood include salmon, cod, and prawns.

ENERGY RESOURCES

For centuries, peat was the primary source of energy across Ireland. People cut the peat by hand and dried it. Then the peat could be burned for heating or cooking. In rural areas, peat-burning stations generated electricity. However, in the 1900s, peat was gradually replaced by fossil fuels such as coal, oil, and natural gas.

IRELAND'S FARMS

Although agriculture is a small part of Ireland's economy today, it is still essential in communities across the country. Most farms are small, family-owned operations. Raising cattle for beef is common in the central regions, while dairy farming is common in the south. Rich grasslands provide fertile pastures for grazing almost year-round. Many farmers in hilly and mountainous regions raise sheep for their wool and meat. Farms in the east and southeast typically grow cereal crops such as wheat and barley.

Today Ireland relies on four primary sources to supply its energy: petroleum, natural gas, renewables, and coal. Petroleum, including crude oil, is the most widely used energy source, providing 49 percent of Ireland's energy in 2023. Natural gas provides about 29 percent of the country's energy supply, while renewables and coal provide 14 and 3 percent, respectively.[13] Peat and nonrenewable wastes provided the country's remaining energy needs.

Because Ireland does not have significant petroleum or natural gas resources, it relies on imports to provide most of its energy. Ireland's oil is almost entirely imported, while a combination of domestic production and imports via a pipeline from Scotland meet its natural gas needs. However, domestic natural gas production is expected to decline as local sources are depleted. As a result, Ireland expects to import more than 90 percent of its natural gas needs by 2030.[14]

Recognizing its reliance on energy imports, Ireland has become one of Europe's leaders in renewable energy technologies. The country's location on the edge of the Atlantic Ocean positions it well for harnessing wind power. In 2023 Ireland's use of renewable energy sources reached record levels. More than half of Ireland's renewable energy came from wind power. Other significant renewable energy sources included biodiesel at 13.6 percent and biomass at 11.2 percent.[15] The country planned to continue increasing its use of renewable energy sources and decreasing its reliance on imported energy. Ireland hoped to be able to produce up to 80 percent of its electricity from renewable energy sources by 2030.[16]

IMPORTS AND EXPORTS

Ireland's main trading partners are the United States and the United Kingdom. Other significant trading partners are in Europe, such as France, Germany, and Belgium. China is another key trading partner. Ireland exports mainly manufactured products such as electrical machinery, chemical products, clothes, beverages, and processed foods. It imports machinery and equipment, chemicals, petroleum, food, and textiles.

TRANSPORTATION

People and goods move throughout Ireland via roads, railways, ports, and airports. Several ports around the country handle goods and passengers traveling to and from Ireland by ship. The Port of Dublin is Ireland's largest port, with 50 percent of the nation's maritime activity flowing through it.[17] Other major Irish ports include the Port of Galway, Port of Shannon Foynes, Port of Bantry Bay, and Port of Cork. In addition to the ports, miles of inland canals and rivers transport people and goods throughout Ireland.

Airports across Ireland welcome travelers and goods. On Ireland's eastern coast, Dublin Airport is the country's busiest, with 28.1 million passengers passing through the airport in 2022. In the south, Ireland's second-largest airport, Cork Airport, saw 2.2 million passengers in 2022.[18]

People dig peat out of the ground and lay it out to dry. In 2022, the rising costs of oil and gas drove more people in Ireland to cut their own peat for fuel.

Connolly Station is the busiest train station in Ireland. It has seven platforms.

Other well-traveled airports are the Shannon, Donegal, Kerry, and Ireland West.

Cars, buses, trucks, and motorcycles travel on the thousands of miles of highways and paved roads across Ireland. The roads connect rural and urban populations. In larger cities such as Dublin, the traffic on the streets can cause congestion and slowdowns. Many people in the city take the Dublin Area Rapid Transport, an electrified commuter rail system, to avoid traffic. Within Dublin, a light-rail tram system called Luas carries passengers to different parts of the city. Many people also ride the Dublin Bus, which provides service within the capital city, while the Irish Bus travels to cities and towns across the country.

Some passengers travel via the Irish Rail to cities and towns throughout the country. There are about 150 stations across the nation.[19] Dublin is the country's railway hub, with its Connolly, Pearse, Heuston, and Tara Street stations servicing almost one-third of all train passengers in Ireland. Outside of Dublin, the cities of Cork, Galway, Limerick, and Waterford also have busy rail stations.

CHAPTER **EIGHT**

IRELAND TODAY

Today, life in Ireland is very similar to life in other European nations and the United States. Agriculture is still important in rural areas, but most Irish people live near urban centers. People in Ireland do many of the same activities that other Europeans or Americans do. They go to school or work, listen to music, watch movies, text friends, and shop online and in stores.

HOMES IN IRELAND

Across Ireland, people live in different styles of housing, from apartments to detached homes. In many places, especially rural areas, stand-alone homes are

People in Ireland enjoy hiking and other outdoor activities in the nation's many natural spaces.

Cobh, Ireland, features terraced houses, including the Deck of Cards houses set on a steep hill.

most common. For these homes, the exterior walls are typically built with concrete blocks. Then, the walls are plastered and painted. Some homes are built with bricks, while older homes used cut stones such as limestone and granite to build walls. In brick homes, the walls may have been covered with thin layers of cut rock in a process called cladding.

Stand-alone homes come in different styles and sizes, with cottages and bungalows being popular. A cottage is a traditional single-story rectangular house. It has front and back doors, and its rooms stretch the entire width of the house. A traditional Irish cottage has thick walls and a steep, thatched roof. Modern cottages may have an upper-level or attic space for additional bedrooms.

The bungalow is the most common house in rural areas of Ireland. This house style usually features one story with or without a partial second floor. A bungalow typically has a low-sloped roof with wide roof edges called eaves that extend beyond the bungalow's walls. Modern bungalows may have two full stories and small dormers on the roof that hold windows.

Semidetached and terraced houses are more common in urban areas because they save space. Semidetached houses share a single wall with another house, while terraced houses resemble town houses in the United States. They are connected by a wall on each side, which creates an unbroken row of houses along a street. Apartments, sometimes called flats, are more common in Ireland's urban areas.

A PINT OF GUINNESS

Many Irish people consider Guinness beer to be Ireland's national drink. Famous worldwide, Guinness is a dark, thick beer that was first brewed in the 1700s at Arthur Guinness's brewery at St. James's Gate in Dublin. With its creamy foam on top, the dark beer has become an Irish staple, served in pubs throughout the country. One can order "a pint of the black stuff," and an Irish bartender will bring a Guinness.

EDUCATION

Ireland's education system is divided into three main stages: primary, secondary, and postsecondary. The law requires children six to 15 years old to attend school. Parents can choose to send their children to state-funded schools or private schools.

Primary education typically begins after a child's fourth birthday but must begin by age six. Most primary schools require students to learn the Irish language unless a special exemption is granted. Students spend several years in primary school before moving to secondary education around age 12.

Irish students choose between three types of secondary schools. Voluntary secondary schools focus on academic education. These schools are usually privately owned but may offer free or subsidized tuition. Voluntary schools are the most common type of secondary school in Ireland today. Some students choose to attend vocational schools and community colleges that are run by the state. These secondary schools focus on vocational education and preparing students for jobs in business, health care, information technology, construction, and more. Other students attend community and comprehensive secondary schools. These schools offer both academic and vocational classes. They are funded by the government and run by local boards.

Students attend secondary school between the ages of 12 and 18. First, they enter a three-year Junior Cycle known as lower secondary. Students in the Junior Cycle study a broad range of subjects to master the foundational knowledge and skills they will need to move on to Senior Cycle education. After three years in the Junior Cycle, students take the Junior Certificate exam.

Around age 15, students enter the Senior Cycle, the upper secondary. Some students choose an optional transition year between the Junior Cycle and Senior Cycle, in which they can gain work experience or learn without worrying about exams. During the last two years of the Senior Cycle, students study several subjects to prepare for one of three state exams: the Leaving Certificate,

Students check their Leaving Certificate exam results online when the results are released.

Leaving Certificate Vocational Program, and Leaving Certificate Applied. Most students take the Leaving Certificate. To prepare, they typically study five or more subjects on which they will be tested. One required subject is the Irish language.

After secondary school, some students attend a university for higher education. Ireland is home to several respected universities. Trinity College Dublin is Ireland's top university and has educated students since 1592. Its campus is in the heart of Dublin, and the university serves more than 18,000 students.[1] Students also have the option to pursue higher education at technology institutes and private colleges.

HOBBIES AND RECREATION

People in Ireland enjoy many hobbies, with traveling, reading, cooking, baking, outdoor activities, and gardening being some of the most popular. Sports are common in local communities, especially rugby, hurling, Gaelic football, and soccer, which is called football in Ireland. Many Irish people also enjoy horse racing at one of Ireland's 26 registered racetracks.[2] Thousands of fans attend major events such as the Galway Races and the Irish Derby each year.

With 300 golf courses across the country, this sport is another popular pastime in Ireland.[3] Challenging links courses along the coastlines provide a spectacular setting for golfers. World-renowned courses such as Ballybunion Golf Club, Portmarnock Golf Club, and the Golf Course at Adare Manor attract locals and tourists alike.

More than 1.2 million people attended horse races at Ireland's racetracks in 2023.[4]

Many people enjoy various outdoor leisure activities among Ireland's beautiful landscapes. Hillwalking, the practice of walking through hilly or mountainous terrain, is popular throughout Ireland. Hiking, bicycling, camping, sailing, kayaking, and canoeing are other outdoor pursuits regularly enjoyed across the country. Surfing has become a popular activity, and Ireland's northwestern coast is a common destination for surfers who want to challenge themselves with the Atlantic Ocean's waves.

GAELIC FOOTBALL

Gaelic football is a popular sport in Ireland. It is similar in several ways to hurling, but Gaelic football players do not use a stick to control the ball. Teams of 15 play on a rectangular grass field with a round ball. Each team attempts to score through H-shaped goals at each end of the field by using their hands and feet to control and pass the ball. The team scores one point if the ball goes over the goal bar. If the ball goes under the bar and into the goalmouth, the team scores three points. The team with the highest score wins the match.

HOLIDAYS AND FESTIVALS

Irish people celebrate holidays and festivals throughout the year. One of the most popular is Saint Patrick's Day, held on March 17 each year. Saint Patrick's Day was initially celebrated to honor the Christian missionary Saint Patrick. Saint Patrick's Day is now a national holiday and a celebration of Irish culture. Communities hold multiday celebrations that include parades, music, carnivals, dance, and art.

On October 31 the traditional Samhain Festival in Dublin celebrates the harvest. Samhain has its roots in Celtic traditions. Today people gather on Dublin's streets for a parade, many dressed in costumes. Throughout the city, parties, fireworks, and other celebrations are held in honor of Samhain. Religious celebrations are also part of daily life in Ireland, where most people practice Catholicism. Christmas, Easter, and Good Friday are some of the major religious holidays that are important in Irish Christian life.

In September, the Lisdoonvarna Matchmaking Festival draws thousands of people to County Clare. In the 1700s a local doctor discovered the health benefits of nearby mineral springs, which relieved symptoms of several conditions. The town's population grew as people traveled to Lisdoonvarna to drink and bathe in the mineral springs. The town's matchmaking tradition emerged as single farmers from rural areas came to town after the harvest in search of wives.

By the 2020s the town's official matchmaker was Willie Daly, whose father and grandfather had held the position before him. Daly runs a local pub and keeps a notebook of people seeking a match. Hopeful people of all ages line up to talk to Daly and hope that he will help them find true love. For those not looking for a match, the festival features dances, Irish music, and a lively time late into the night.

BLOOMSDAY FESTIVAL

Every year on June 16, Ireland celebrates the Bloomsday Festival to honor Irish author James Joyce. The festival is named after Leopold Bloom, one of the characters in Joyce's famous novel *Ulysses*. Throughout Dublin, crowds gather to watch people re-create scenes from *Ulysses*. Many people dress in character, either as the author himself or as characters from his famous novels.

Willie Daly's bar is called the Matchmaker Bar. The Lisdoonvarna Matchmaking Festival runs through the entire month of September.

Many young people from regions in Ireland where Irish is the main language cannot afford housing there, forcing them to leave. Some protest to ask the government to make housing in these places more affordable.

DEALING WITH CHALLENGES

Like every nation in the world, Ireland faces challenges. One of the biggest problems in recent years is the shortage of affordable housing for the country's growing population. Rapidly rising rent costs have made many homes and apartments in Irish cities such as Dublin unaffordable.

In Dublin, the average rent doubled between 2013 and 2023. Unable to afford rent, two-thirds of young adults in Dublin live at home with family, a rate much higher than the average European rate of 42 percent.[5] Analysts say that the failure of the Irish government over the years to invest in low-cost housing has led to the current housing crisis. The Irish government is reviewing the private rental market to determine the best way to provide safe, affordable housing for people across Ireland.

Another challenge facing Ireland is the rising cost of living. Like many countries worldwide, Ireland experienced a period of high inflation between 2020 and 2022. Although the country's inflation rate has dropped from its peak in 2022, prices remain high in Ireland. Many Irish people are still finding it difficult to pay for the necessities of daily life.

Ireland and its people have faced many challenges, yet they continue looking toward the future. In the mid-1800s, Ireland's population peaked before the Great Famine caused many deaths and a wave of emigration. Although Ireland's population has not recovered to prefamine levels, it is growing and thriving today. With the country's natural beauty, heritage, culture, and traditions, the future looks bright for Ireland and its people.

ESSENTIAL **FACTS**

OFFICIAL NAME: REPUBLIC OF IRELAND

GEOGRAPHY

Area: 27,133 square miles (70,273 sq km)

Highest Elevation: Carrantuohill at 3,415 feet (1,041 m)

Lowest Elevation: Atlantic Ocean at 0 feet (0 m)

PEOPLE

Population: 5.2 million (2024 est.)

Most Populous City: Dublin (1.27 million)

Ethnic Groups: Irish, other white, Asian, Black, other, Irish Travellers

Religions: Christianity, Islam, other

GOVERNMENT

Type of Government: Parliamentary republic

Capital: Dublin

Head of State: President

Head of Government: Taoiseach (prime minister)

Legislature: Bicameral Oireachtas (parliament), with a Seanad Éireann and Dáil Éireann

ECONOMY

Currency: Euro

Major Industries: Services, pharmaceuticals, chemicals, computer hardware and software, food products, beverages and brewing, medical devices

Natural Resources: Natural gas, peat, copper, lead, zinc, silver, barite, gypsum, limestone, dolomite

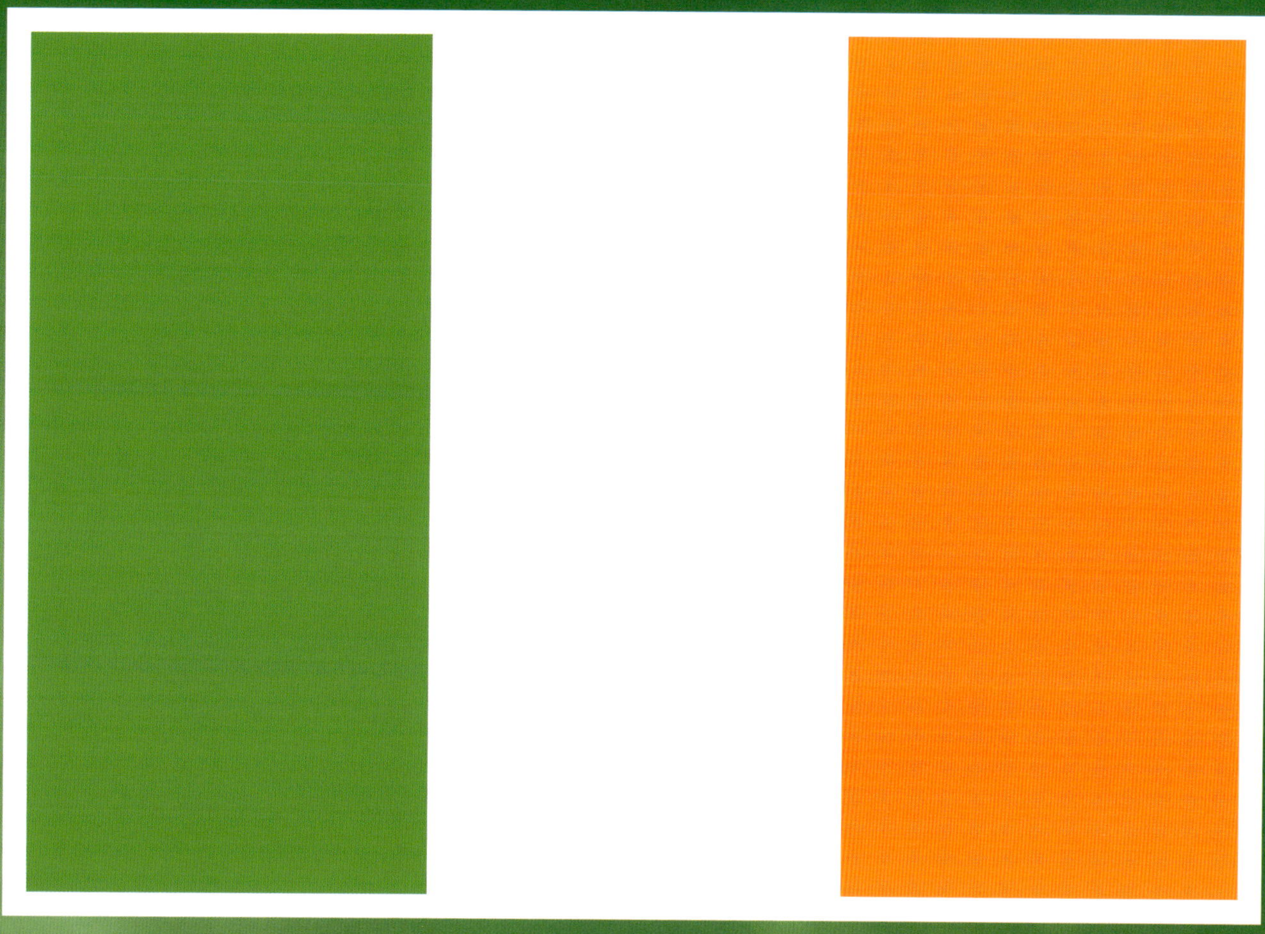

NATIONAL SYMBOLS

National Anthem: "Amhrán na bhFiann" ("The Soldier's Song")

National Bird: Lapwing

National Plant: Shamrock

GLOSSARY

archaeologist
A person who studies human history by examining artifacts and other physical remains.

cleric
A priest or religious leader.

conservative
Believing in small government and established social, economic, and political traditions and practices.

export
To sell goods to another country.

famine
An extreme scarcity of food.

fen
A type of low-lying wetland that forms peat.

habitat
The natural environment of an organism.

heath
An area of land where grass and small plants grow, with few trees or bushes.

import
To buy goods from another country.

missionary
A person sent to promote a religion, often Christianity, or to operate a service such as a school or hospital under that religion, usually where that religion is not widely practiced.

monk
A man who has joined a religious order and has usually taken vows of poverty, chastity, and obedience.

reservoir
A human-made lake for storing water for people to use.

subsidized
Describing when a third party has paid part of the cost of something in order to lower the price for the purchaser.

ADDITIONAL **RESOURCES**

SELECTED BIBLIOGRAPHY

Ireland in Brief: A General Overview of Ireland's Political, Economic and Cultural Life. Department of Foreign Affairs and Trade, Aug. 2014, dfa.ie. Accessed 15 Oct. 2024.

McGreevy, Ronan. "'More Than a Quarter' of Species in Ireland at Risk of Extinction." *Irish Times*, 24 Sept. 2022, irishtimes.com. Accessed 15 Oct. 2024.

Wilson, Neil, et al. *Ireland*. Lonely Planet, 2020.

FURTHER READINGS

Deary, Terry. *Ireland*. Scholastic, 2022.

Ireland. DK, 2024.

Mooney, Carla. *United Kingdom*. Abdo, 2023.

ONLINE RESOURCES

To learn more about Ireland, please visit **abdobooklinks.com** or scan this QR code. These links are routinely monitored and updated to provide the most current information available.

MORE INFORMATION

For more information on this subject, contact or visit the following organizations:

EPIC The Irish Emigration Museum

CHQ, Custom House Quay
Dublin 1, D01 R9Y0
epicchq.com

The Irish Emigration Museum is an interactive museum that brings Irish history to life and explores the stories of Irish emigrants worldwide.

Houses of the Oireachtas

Leinster House
Kildare St.
Dublin 2, D02 XR20
oireachtas.ie

The Oireachtas is the parliament of Ireland. Its website has a "Visit and Learn" section that explains the history and operation of the Irish parliament.

National Museum of Ireland—Archaeology

Kildare St.
Dublin 2, D02 FH48
museum.ie/en-IE/Museums/Archaeology

The National Museum of Ireland—Archaeology is the national repository for all archaeological objects found in Ireland and has more than two million artifacts.

SOURCE **NOTES**

CHAPTER 1. A TOUR OF IRELAND

1. "Almost 35 Million Passengers through Ireland's Two Busiest Airports in 2023." *daa*, 24 Jan. 2024, daa.ie. Accessed 3 Jan. 2025.
2. John O'Beirne Ranelagh. "Dublin." *Britannica*, 3 Jan. 2025, britannica.com. Accessed 3 Jan. 2025.
3. "About Us." *Dublin Port*, n.d., dublinport.ie. Accessed 3 Jan. 2025.
4. Neil Wilson et al. *Ireland*. Lonely Planet, 2020. 524–525.
5. "Ha'penny Bridge." *Bridges of Dublin*, n.d., bridgesofdublin.ie. Accessed 3 Jan. 2025.
6. Wilson et al., *Ireland*, 524–525.
7. "World Heritage List." *UNESCO World Heritage Convention*, n.d., whc.unesco.org. Accessed 3 Jan. 2025.
8. "Ireland." *CIA World Factbook*, 30 Dec. 2024, cia.gov. Accessed 3 Jan. 2025.
9. "Ireland."

CHAPTER 2. GEOGRAPHY

1. Sean Kay et al. "Ireland." *Britannica*, 3 Jan. 2025, britannica.com. Accessed 3 Jan. 2025.
2. "Home Page." *Ireland's Dingle Peninsula*, n.d., dingle-peninsula.ie. Accessed 3 Jan. 2025.
3. "Islands of Ireland." *Ireland Travel Guide*, n.d., myirelandtour.com. Accessed 3 Jan. 2025.
4. "Ring of Kerry." *Tourism Ireland*, n.d., ireland.com. Accessed 3 Jan. 2025.
5. "Limestone Lowland Landscapes." *Ask about Ireland*, n.d., askaboutireland.ie. Accessed 3 Jan. 2025.
6. Caroline Oberheu. "The Tallest Mountains in Ireland." *WorldAtlas*, 3 Sept. 2019, worldatlas.com. Accessed 3 Jan. 2025.
7. "Carrantuohill." *Britannica*, 25 Apr. 2011, britannica.com. Accessed 3 Jan. 2025.
8. "MacGillycuddy's Reeks." *PeakVisor*, n.d., peakvisor.com. Accessed 3 Jan. 2025.
9. "Mountains of Ireland." *Ireland Walking Guide*, n.d., theirelandwalkingguide.com. Accessed 3 Jan. 2025.
10. "Wicklow Mountains." *Irish Tourism*, n.d., irishtourism.com. Accessed 3 Jan. 2025.
11. Kay et al., "Ireland."
12. Ferdinand Bada. "The Largest Lakes in Ireland." *WorldAtlas*, 18 July 2018, worldatlas.com. Accessed 3 Jan. 2025.
13. "National Lake Monitoring Programme." *Environmental Protection Agency*, n.d., epa.ie. Accessed 3 Jan. 2025.
14. "Lough Corrib." *Discover Ireland*, n.d., discoverireland.ie. Accessed 3 Jan. 2025.
15. "Primary Seniors—Mountains, Rivers & Lakes." *Ordnance Survey Ireland*, n.d., web.archive.org. Accessed 3 Jan. 2025.
16. Benjamin Elisha Sawe. "The Longest Rivers in Ireland." *WorldAtlas*, 26 June 2018, worldatlas.com. Accessed 3 Jan. 2025.
17. Irish Peatland Conservation Council. "Boglands." *Peatlands*, n.d., thepeatlands.ie. Accessed 3 Jan. 2025.
18. "Family Farming Knowledge Platform: Ireland." *Food and Agricultural Organization of the United Nations*, n.d., fao.org. Accessed 3 Jan. 2025.
19. "Ireland." *CIA World Factbook*, 30 Dec. 2024, cia.gov. Accessed 3 Jan. 2025.
20. "Irish Weather and Climate." *Ireland's Blue Book*, n.d., irelands-blue-book.ie. Accessed 3 Jan. 2025.
21. "Irish Weather and Climate."
22. "Best Cliffs in Ireland." *Doolin Ferry Co.*, n.d., doolinferry.com. Accessed 3 Jan. 2025.
23. "Ireland: Current Climate > Climatology." *Climate Change Knowledge Portal*, n.d., climateknowledgeportal.worldbank.org. Accessed 3 Jan. 2025.
24. "Forests of Ireland." *Forestry Focus*, n.d., forestryfocus.ie. Accessed 3 Jan. 2025.

CHAPTER 3. PLANTS AND ANIMALS

1. "Ireland—Country Profile." *Convention on Biological Diversity*, n.d., cbd.int. Accessed 3 Jan. 2025.
2. "History of Forestry in Ireland." *Teagasc*, n.d., teagasc.ie. Accessed 3 Jan. 2025.
3. "History of Forestry in Ireland."
4. "Ireland Has Lost Almost All of Its Native Forests—Here's How to Bring Them Back." *Planetary Press*, 7 Mar. 2023, theplanetarypress.com. Accessed 3 Jan. 2025.
5. "Ireland." *Biodiversity Information System for Europe*, n.d., biodiversity.europa.eu. Accessed 3 Jan. 2025.
6. "Grasslands." *Irish Native Rare Breed Society*, n.d., inrbs.ie. Accessed 3 Jan. 2025.
7. "Ireland," *Biodiversity Information System for Europe*.
8. "Species List." *Irish Wildlife Trust*, n.d., iwt.ie. Accessed 3 Jan. 2025.
9. Ferdia Marnell, Naomi Kingston, and Declan Looney. *Ireland: Red List No. 3: Terrestrial Mammals*. National Parks and Wildlife Service, Department of the Environment, Heritage and Local Government, 2009, npws.ie. Accessed 3 Jan. 2025.
10. "Species List."
11. "Insects." *National Museum of Ireland*, n.d., museum.ie. Accessed 3 Jan. 2025.
12. "Our Guide to Ireland's National Parks." *Ireland Chauffeur Travel*, n.d., irelandchauffeurtravel.com. Accessed 3 Jan. 2025.
13. "Where Nature Speaks." *National Parks*, n.d., nationalparks.ie. Accessed 3 Jan. 2025.
14. Ronan McGreevy. "'More Than a Quarter' of Species in Ireland at Risk of Extinction." *Irish Times*, 24 Sept. 2022, irishtimes.com. Accessed 3 Jan. 2025.

CHAPTER 4. HISTORY

1. Camila. "15 Best Castles in Ireland You Should Visit." *Nordic Visitor Blog*, 10 Aug. 2024, nordicvisitor.com. Accessed 3 Jan. 2025.
2. "Learn about the Great Hunger." *Ireland's Great Hunger Museum*, n.d., ighm.org. Accessed 3 Jan. 2025.
3. "Learn about the Great Hunger."
4. *Ireland in Brief*. Department of Foreign Affairs and Trade, n.d., dfa.ie. Accessed 3 Jan. 2025.
5. "Irish Emigration to America." *National Museum of Ireland*, n.d., museum.ie. Accessed 3 Jan. 2025.
6. "Irish-Catholic Immigration to America." *Library of Congress*, n.d., loc.gov. Accessed 3 Jan. 2025.
7. "Irish Emigration to America."
8. "The Northern Ireland Conflict—Peace by Piece." *Association for Diplomatic Studies and Training*, n.d., adst.org. Accessed 3 Jan. 2025.

SOURCE NOTES CONTINUED

CHAPTER 5. PEOPLE AND CULTURE

1. "Ireland." *CIA World Factbook*, 30 Dec. 2024, cia.gov. Accessed 3 Jan. 2025.
2. "Ireland Population (Live)." *Worldometer*, n.d., worldometers.info. Accessed 3 Jan. 2025.
3. "Country Comparisons: Median Age." *CIA World Factbook*, 2024, cia.gov. Accessed 3 Jan. 2025.
4. "Country Comparisons: Birth Rate." *CIA World Factbook*, 2024, cia.gov. Accessed 3 Jan. 2025.
5. "Ireland," *CIA World Factbook*.
6. "Ireland Population (Live)."
7. "European Countries by Population (2025)." *Worldometer*, n.d., worldometers.info. Accessed 3 Jan. 2025.
8. "Ireland," *CIA World Factbook*.
9. "Census of Population 2022—Summary Results." *An Phríomh-Oifig Staidrimh (Central Statistics Office)*, n.d., cso.ie. Accessed 3 Jan. 2025.
10. "Ireland," *CIA World Factbook*.
11. "Ireland," *CIA World Factbook*.
12. Michael Connolly, Chris James, and Luke Murtagh. "Reflections on Recent Developments in the Governance of Schools in Ireland and the Role of the Church." *Sage Journals*, 6 June 2023, journals.sagepub.com. Accessed 3 Jan. 2025.
13. *Barometer 2023 Research Paper Series: A Detailed Overview of the Drinkaware Barometer 2023 Findings*. Drinkaware, Apr. 2024, drugsandalcohol.ie. Accessed 27 Jan. 2025.
14. "What Is Hurling?" *Experience Gaelic Games*, n.d., experiencegaelicgames.com. Accessed 3 Jan. 2025.

CHAPTER 6. POLITICS

1. "TDs & Senators." *Tithe an Oireachtais (Houses of the Oireachtas)*, n.d., oireachtas.ie. Accessed 27 Jan. 2025.
2. "Latest Polling Data and Election Polls for Fianna Fáil." *PolitPro*, n.d., politpro.eu. Accessed 3 Jan. 2025.
3. "Latest Polling Data and Election Polls for Fine Gael." *PolitPro*, n.d., politpro.eu. Accessed 3 Jan. 2025.
4. "Latest Polling Data and Election Polls for Sinn Féin." *PolitPro*, n.d., politpro.eu. Accessed 3 Jan. 2025.
5. "Local Government." *Citizens Information*, n.d., citizensinformation.ie. Accessed 3 Jan. 2025.
6. "Defence Forces: Dáil Éireann Debate, Tuesday—23 January 2024." *Tithe an Oireachtais (Houses of the Oireachtas)*, 23 Jan. 2024, oireachtas.ie. Accessed 3 Jan. 2025.

CHAPTER 7. ECONOMICS

1. "Ireland GDP: Summary." *Trading Economics*, n.d., tradingeconomics.com. Accessed 3 Jan. 2025.
2. "The World's Largest Economies." *WorldData.info*, n.d., worlddata.info. Accessed 3 Jan. 2025.
3. "Indicators of Economy in Ireland." *WorldData.info*, n.d., worlddata.info. Accessed 3 Jan. 2025.
4. Aaron O'Neill. "Ireland: Distribution of Gross Domestic Product (GDP) across Economic Sectors from 2012 to 2022." *Statista*, 4 July 2024, statista.com. Accessed 3 Jan. 2025.
5. "Ireland: Economic and Political Overview." *Lloyds Bank*, July 2024, lloydsbanktrade.com. Accessed 3 Jan. 2025.
6. "Inbound Tourism Annual 2023." *An Phríomh-Oifig Staidrimh (Central Statistics Office)*, 19 June 2024, cso.ie. Accessed 3 Jan. 2025.
7. "Ireland: Economic and Political Overview."
8. "Ireland: Economic and Political Overview."
9. "Ireland." *CIA World Factbook*, 30 Dec. 2024, cia.gov. Accessed 3 Jan. 2025.
10. "Ireland—Country Commercial Guide." *International Trade Administration*, 25 Jan. 2024, trade.gov. Accessed 3 Jan. 2025.
11. "Inbound Tourism Annual 2023."
12. "Fisheries in Ireland." *European Commission*, 31 May 2024, ireland.representation.ec.europa.eu. Accessed 3 Jan. 2025.
13. *First Look: Ireland's Energy Supply and Security of Supply in 2023: Part A—Key Insights*. Sustainable Energy Authority of Ireland, July 2024, seai.ie. Accessed 3 Jan. 2025.
14. Sarah Mooney. "Explained: Where Does Ireland Get Its Energy From?" *BreakingNews.ie*, 10 July 2022, breakingnews.ie. Accessed 3 Jan. 2025.
15. *First Look*.
16. "How Ireland Is Becoming a Leader in Renewable Energy Technology." *Reuters Plus*, n.d., plus.reuters.com. Accessed 3 Jan. 2025.
17. Zahra Ahmed. "7 Major Ports of Ireland." *Marine Insight*, 16 Dec. 2022, marineinsight.com. Accessed 3 Jan. 2025.
18. Keith O'Hara. "International Airports in Ireland (Map + Key Info)." *Irish Road Trip*, 6 Aug. 2024, theirishroadtrip.com. Accessed 3 Jan. 2025.
19. "Find an Iarnród Éireann Station." *Iarnród Éireann (Irish Rail)*, n.d., irishrail.ie. Accessed 3 Jan. 2025.

CHAPTER 8. IRELAND TODAY

1. "About Trinity College Dublin, the University of Dublin." *QS Top Universities*, n.d., topuniversities.com. Accessed 3 Jan. 2025.
2. "Horse Racing in Ireland—the Biggest Events." *Horsevents.co.uk*, 14 Aug. 2024, horsevents.co.uk. Accessed 3 Jan. 2025.
3. "Ireland Golf Courses." *Discovering Ireland Vacations*, n.d., discoveringireland.com. Accessed 3 Jan. 2025.
4. *Factbook 2023 Every Racing Moment*. Horse Racing Ireland, n.d., hri.ie. Accessed 3 Jan 2025.
5. Megan Specia. "'The Social Contract Has Been Completely Ruptured': Ireland's Housing Crisis." *New York Times*, 15 Jan. 2024, nytimes.com. Accessed 3 Jan. 2025.

INDEX

ABOUT THE **AUTHOR**

CARLA MOONEY

Carla Mooney is a graduate of the University of Pennsylvania with a degree in economics. Today, she writes for young people and is the author of many books for young adults and children. Mooney enjoys traveling to new places around the world and has visited Ireland twice.